Buying Software –
A Best Practice Approach

London: TSO

Published by TSO (The Stationery Office) and available from:

Online
www.tso.co.uk/bookshop

Mail, Telephone, Fax & E-mail
TSO
PO Box 29, Norwich, NR3 1GN
Telephone orders/General enquiries: 0870 600 5522
Fax orders: 0870 600 5533
E-mail: book.orders@tso.co.uk
Textphone: 0870 240 3701

TSO Shops
123 Kingsway, London, WC2B 6PQ
020 7242 6393 Fax 020 7242 6394
68-69 Bull Street, Birmingham B4 6AD
0121 236 9696 Fax 0121 236 9699
9-21 Princess Street, Manchester M60 8AS
0161 834 7201 Fax 0161 833 0634
16 Arthur Street, Belfast BT1 4GD
028 9023 8451 Fax 028 9023 5401
18-19 High Street, Cardiff CF10 1PT
029 2039 5548 Fax 029 2038 4347
71 Lothian Road, Edinburgh EH3 9AZ
0870 606 5566 Fax 0870 606 5588

TSO Accredited Agents
(see Yellow Pages)

and through good booksellers

A CIP catalogue record for this book is available from the British Library

A Library of Congress CIP catalogue record has been applied for

First published 2004

ISBN 0 11 330918 X

Printed in the United Kingdom by The Stationery Office Limited   08/04 989423 19585

CONTENTS

PREFACE

The rate of investment made in software by both the private and public sectors rises steadily each year. Software procurement is increasing as a proportion of total IT expenditure, and it seems we can look forward to the day when the hardware element of IT investments will be trivial compared to software.

Software is a critical part of everyday business life, and increasingly important for leisure and personal use, too. Yet there is very little published guidance on how to maximise benefit when selecting software. For minor, off-the-shelf purchases, this may be just a matter of finding the cheapest vendor. However, when selecting or bespoking major software applications, this mindset is simply not robust enough to ensure that benefits and value for money are achieved.

This book describes the best practice general approach to selecting software, and suggests a structured process that will ensure maximum benefit. The approach is based on best practices from the private sector, and integrates the best project management methods with software selection. The guidance is also complementary to OGC Best Practice guides for other aspects of IT.

The advice given is just as valuable for smaller software procurements as for large ones, with suggestions given on when fast-tracking is possible. We urge and encourage you to consider the advice within this book, and hope that it helps both public and private sectors to obtain effective and beneficial software.

ACKNOWLEDGEMENTS

The author would like to acknowledge the help and support of Stephen Barney, Joyce Brook and Tim Veale in the development of this book. Their efforts were much appreciated and valued.

1

INTRODUCTION TO THE SOFTWARE SELECTION PROCESS

Most people would not spend their hard-earned money on a new car if they did not know what type of vehicle they wanted, or what they needed the car to do. They would not buy a racing car if they needed a local runabout. It is likely that they would consider the following factors in a rational way, and discuss them with the key affected stakeholders (such as their partner):

- the requirements the car must meet
- the criteria on which decisions will be made
- the features they would like the car to have
- the ways in which life would be better if they had the car
- the cost of ownership
- how to fund the lifetime costs.

Most people buy cars with far more rationality than most organisations buy software. Many software purchases, even big ones, are made without rational consideration of all the relevant factors by all the relevant people. The results are wasted money, lost benefits and damaged careers.

The money wasted in the UK alone on inappropriate software purchases is probably enough to buy 30,000 brand new family cars each year.

Much of the wasted money and resources could be avoided by taking a project-based approach to selecting the right software. The Software Selection Process (SSP) described in this book provides a flexible framework in which to do this, based on tried and tested project management principles.

1.1 Why this book is necessary

- When implementing new software tools or applications people often end up with:
  - systems that do not meet requirements
  - personal and organisational pain
  - extra cost and delays
  - user and/or client complaints
  - having to start over again.

- Software is becoming ubiquitous in business operations, and is no longer only the domain of IT experts. IT people have a major role in software selection, but business process experts own most of the requirements and long-term benefits.

- Business and process experts may lack confidence and insight into what the important technological factors are. SSP lays out a framework for capturing *all* the factors that should go into decisions, and ensures *all* stakeholders are represented.

- A project-based approach to maximising benefits from new software encourages:
  - satisfaction of business needs
  - appropriate levels of control and reporting
  - reduced cost and increased benefit
  - fewer surprises.

1.2   Who should read this book?

This book will prove useful to the following types of people:

- business managers who pay for and benefit from software
- senior stakeholders wishing to find a voice in software selection or avoid high-profile software disasters
- project managers responsible for organising selection and procurement exercises
- sales and marketing staff within software suppliers, who can learn more about their clients' selection process and value issues
- IT managers wishing to add more objectivity to cross-functional software decisions.

> Software purchases should take lifetime impact into account today, so that there are far fewer surprises tomorrow.

SSP is a series of suggested steps to help organisations maximise the benefit from implementing new software tools or applications. The approach includes the entire sequence of activities, from first idea through to successful implementation, plus post-implementation review. This is shown diagrammatically in Figure 1.1.

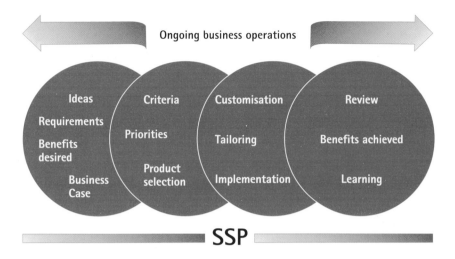

Figure 1.1 – The context of the Software Selection Process

1.3   Why bother?

1.3.1 Key software facts

The following statistics demonstrate how important software is to both public and private sector organisations, and how wasteful inappropriate software can be.

- In 2002 the UK is thought to have spent around €13 billion on software, of which the public sector spent €2 billion.

- The public sector spends around €1100 per employee per annum on software alone.

- In 2002 software accounted for around 14% of total IT expenditure. By 2006 this will have risen to 25%.

- Software expenditure is expected to grow by 11% to 15% **per annum** through to 2006, about five times faster than inflation.

- Public sector expenditure on software is rising faster than private sector at all stages in the economic cycle.

- In 2006 the UK software market will be worth around €23 billion per annum.

Effective software can be an enormous benefit to an organisation, opening new markets, creating new products and enabling step change improvements in the efficiency of business processes. In contrast, ineffective software can waste precious time, money and other resources, leading to frustration, lost business and failure to meet business objectives.

3

Assuming that 10% of software expenditure fails to meet business needs, the UK wasted around €1.3 billion in 2002, of which the public sector wasted around €200 million. If nothing is done to arrest this, by 2006 the UK will be wasting around €2.4 billion per annum, of which the public sector will be wasting around €400 million.

Reducing the assumed expenditure on inappropriate software from 10% to 7% would save the private sector around €400 million, and the public sector around €60 million **per annum** in reduced purchase costs alone. The knock-on impact of inappropriate software, such as lost productivity, lost benefits and low staff morale will be many times larger.

Accurate figures on the level of inappropriate software expenditure are very hard to obtain, and one can debate whether the assumptions made above are correct. Nevertheless, the money spent on software each year in the UK is huge.

People involved in selecting and implementing new software will wish to use SSP to avoid the avoidable problems, and manage the risk that the new software does not deliver the expected benefits. This will be good for the business, and good for personal reputations.

> SSP is designed to significantly reduce expenditure on inappropriate software.
>
> SSP delivers two big advantages:
>
> - it eliminates expenditure on the wrong software
> - it increases benefits from selecting the right software.

1.3.2 Benefits of using SSP

SSP is based upon best-practice principles, with emphasis on practical application and common sense.

Organising software selection exercises along project management lines has many advantages:

- focus, effectiveness and efficiency
- management by fact and clear governance
- business needs and benefits clearly articulated
- stakeholder involvement and commitment
- appropriate handling of risks and issues
- structured and auditable approach.

Pragmatic benefits from a project-based approach are:

- clarity of purpose
- faster progress
- better cross-functional communications
- decision-making that includes technical and operational views.

It is also the case that by using SSP to link software purchases to business objectives, unnecessary duplication of effort and expenditure can be eliminated. If requirements are coordinated it is easier to spot situations such as two departments both procuring similar software (e.g. accounting systems) from different suppliers when one combined system would do.

1.3.3 Disadvantages and how to avoid them

There are three potential disadvantages of using SSP, each of which is addressed below.

1.3.3.1 Inappropriate scaling and perceived bureaucracy

Only the largest and most expensive software selection exercises would need to consider in depth all the factors outlined in this book. Organisations must decide which topics are most important to the business, and focus an appropriate amount of effort in those directions. Failure to do this will lead to a bureaucratic approach, slow progress and poor buy-in from staff.

1.3.3.2 Paralysis by analysis

An important part of any project-based approach to organisational change is planning – early work to identify the goal posts and activities required. However, if clear leadership is not provided, excessive analysis can become the goal in its own right, and no real progress ever gets made. The solution is to ensure that progress can be monitored, and that there is appropriate analysis without paralysis.

1.3.3.3 Lack of buy-in

Some people may perceive a project-based approach to software selection to be unnecessary, bureaucratic or over-analytical. The key point here is to ensure that levels of analysis and control are appropriate to the business needs, working culture, cost and expected benefits from use of the software.

Before paying for a new family car most people would give rational consideration to the style, features, performance, economy and number of seats, taking into account the needs of children, parents, grandparents, etc. This ensures that hard-earned money is not wasted and the car meets the requirements. Sometimes compromises need to be made by some interested parties, in the general interests of the group as a whole.

Businesses need to make similar choices. If organisers of software procurements can explain to people why analysis and control are needed, and how stakeholder voices will be heard, people will usually become supporters of the process.

> Do the needs of the many outweigh the needs of the few, or the needs of the few outweigh the needs of the many?
>
> The SSP Criteria and Weighting Model provides an objective method of evaluating and weighing the needs of different groups, so that this question can be answered.

1.4   What is SSP?

SSP consists of four major processes further subdivided into 12 steps, and takes a project-based approach to defining the decision-making criteria. All steps should be tailored to fit local culture and be appropriate to the size and risk of each software selection exercise. Smaller exercises should still consider each of these steps, although it may not be necessary to undertake each one formally.

This book is designed to meet the needs of a number of different audiences. Any one individual may not need to read or study all sections. The guidance is aimed at both public and private sector organisations. Public sector organisations will find SSP aligns with existing UK Government best practice guidelines, e.g. Gateway reviews, procurement expertise, risk management, MSP programme management and PRINCE2 project management.

The book is aimed at people who will be taking an active part in a software selection exercise, or who wish to maximise benefits from a new software application or tool. This would include senior managers who own the business requirements, senior stakeholders, project managers responsible for day-to-day requirements definition and selection, as well as auditors, quality assurance people and team members.

Line managers who have been asked to provide staff to assist with the software selection exercise might like to read Chapter 2, *An overview of the Software Selection Process*.

This book is structured as follows:

- Chapter 1: Introduction
- Chapters 2–6: Descriptions of the four major process steps in SSP
- Chapters 7–13: General guidance on criteria and weightings.

Chapter 1: **Introduction to the Software Selection Process**

The background and concepts behind SSP.

Chapter 2: **An overview of the Software Selection Process**

A short summary of the four major steps in SSP, why they are there, and how they work. Includes a 60 second summary of SSP.

Chapter 3: **The Preparation Process**

A detailed description of how to ensure that the requirements, benefits and Business Case are justifiable and objective. Also included is a framework for control and organisation of people, ensuring that all stakeholder groups are represented at technical, business process and managerial decision-making levels.

Chapter 4: **The Criteria and Weighting Process**

A detailed description of how to capture criteria that the software must fulfil in order to meet requirements and deliver benefits from live usage. Each criterion is weighted according to its importance to the business.

Chapter 5: **The Selection Process**

A detailed description of how to ensure that alternative solutions and approaches are considered, plus objective comparison of different solutions. Strengths and weaknesses of each are revealed, so that rational decisions can be made on which options to procure, plus any tailoring required.

Chapter 6: **The Implementation Process**

A detailed description of how to ensure continuity from selection through implementation, to ensure that expected benefits are genuinely being achieved after a period of use. Hooks into organisation learning are provided.

Chapter 7: **Introduction to key criteria and weightings**

An introduction to the remaining chapters, which describe generic factors to be taken into account in software selection exercises. Chapter 7 explains how to use the information, and suggested weighting criteria are described from Chapter 8 onwards.

Chapter 8: **Criteria and Weighting – Strategic factors**

This chapter describes strategic organisational factors and their importance to the Business Case, Approach and Stakeholder roles, along with a Criteria and Weighting Model.

Chapter 9: **Criteria and Weighting – Commercial factors**

This chapter describes commercial factors and their importance to the Business Case, Approach and Stakeholder roles, along with a Criteria and Weighting Model.

Chapter 10: **Criteria and Weighting – User factors**

This chapter describes user factors and their importance to the Business Case, Approach and Stakeholder roles, along with a Criteria and Weighting Model.

Chapter 11: **Criteria and Weighting – Training factors**

This chapter describes training factors and their importance to the Business Case, Approach and Stakeholder roles, along with a Criteria and Weighting Model.

Chapter 12: **Criteria and Weighting – Data and security factors**

This chapter describes data and security factors and their importance to the Business Case, Approach and Stakeholder roles, along with a Criteria and Weighting Model.

Chapter 13: **Criteria and Weighting – Roll-out and run-time factors**

This chapter describes implementation factors and their importance to the Business Case, Approach and Stakeholder roles, along with a Criteria and Weighting Model.

Appendix A: **Glossary**

Meanings of frequently used terms within this book.

Appendix B: **Further information**

Address and contact details of other relevant sources of information.

1.4.1 Scope

SSP is not intended to cover every single aspect of selection and implementation. Requirements and Implementation Processes will vary from one organisation to another, as will detailed criteria, weightings and tools.

Within the scope of SSP are:

- the management of software selection activities
- stakeholder representation
- a factual basis for management decision-making
- generic guidance on criteria
- weighting models and evaluation of different options

- feedback during implementation
- post-implementation review.

A key part of SSP is the development of a Criteria and Weighting Model, used to evaluate different software options against a wide range of criteria and business requirements. This book provides general guidance and principles when selecting any software applications or tools, and suggests generic areas from which criteria can be drawn.

A supplementary volume to this book has been published, which provides a fully worked Criteria and Weighting Model for selecting tools which support either PRINCE2 (Managing Successful Projects) or MSP (Managing Successful Programmes) methodologies from the UK Office of Government Commerce (OGC). Volume 2 contains guidance and specific criteria for evaluating whether PRINCE 2 and MSP tools can generally promote or enforce adoption of those methods in an organisation.

Key sources of guidance are:

- **OGC Successful Delivery Tool-kit**
  This tool-kit brings together policy and best practice in a single point of reference. It describes proven good practice for procurement, programmes, projects, risk and service management. It gives practical advice on improvement.

- **M_o_R (Management of Risk)**
  A new definition of best practice in corporate risk management, covering strategic, programme, project and operational aspects. M_o_R builds on previous UK Government Orange Book guidance and addresses many of the needs stated in the UK Stock Exchange Combined Code on corporate governance.

- **MSP (Managing Successful Programmes)**
  Best practice in programme management. An essential link between the desire for strategic changes and the need to give projects clear objectives.

- **PRINCE2 (Managing Successful Projects)**
  Best practice in project management – using projects with clear objectives as a way to deliver tactical change effectively.

- **ITIL (IT Infrastructure Library)**
  Best practice in the use of IT in business.

1.4.2 SSP and the software lifecycle

SSP acknowledges the full lifecycle of software. However, it concentrates on the period from the initial identification of a requirement, through to a selected solution (see Figure 1.2).

Unless the software is 100% bespoke, it will have been in existence before software selection began. Typically the software will also be in use long after the selection and implementation exercise has been completed, with benefits being achieved throughout its ongoing use.

Organisations should baseline benefits before commencing change, so that progress can be tracked from a known base. Review of actual benefits achieved after a period of use should also take place, so that corrective action can be taken if expectations are not being met.

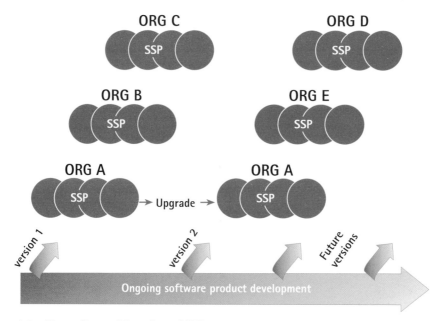

Figure 1.2 – The software lifecycle and SSP

1.4.3 SSP and the local organisation

Most organisations will already have procedures and working practices in place for making business decisions and functional changes. If these are already working satisfactorily then there is little justification for re-inventing them.

UK public sector organisations may already be using the Gateway review process as a basis for managing change. The Gateway process is a general purpose approach to change management and procurement. SSP is focused purely on change through selection of new software.

SSP maps against the Gateway process as shown in Table 1.1.

Table 1.1 – SSP and the Gateway process

Public sector Gateway process	SSP
Gate 0 Strategic assessment Alignment with strategy Early views on Business Case Set up stakeholder representation	*Preparation Process* Business Objectives Stakeholder Analysis Planning
Gate 1 Business justification Outline Business Case Level of risk is appropriate	*Preparation Process* Initial Business Case Functional Analysis Benefits Analysis
Gate 2 Procurement strategy Robustness of procurement Controls, funding, responsibilities Procurement expertise M_O_R – risk management	*Criteria and Weighting Process* Criteria Definition Weighting Definition Business Review
Gate 3 Investment decision Confirmation of Business Case Risk assessment Green book – Investment Appraisal Procurement rules Confirmation of feasible solution	*Selection Process* Market Analysis and Final Approach Scoring Decisions and Procurement
Gate 4 Readiness for service Confirmation of robustness before implementation	*Implementation Process*
Gate 5 Benefits evaluation Benefit review after a period of use	*Implementation Process*

SSP should not exist in isolation – it should be tailored and dovetailed with existing working practices. Where there is lack of clarity SSP can be used as documented. In other cases, it may only be necessary to re-emphasise the key messages of:

- clear decision-making body
- clear responsibility for day-to-day control
- stakeholder involvement
- use of the Business Case as basis for weighting of criteria and decision-making.

Since software is an aspect of IT, any software selection exercise should take due account of any IT strategies, policies and procedures in place (see Figure 1.3). It would be prudent to review such policies before making major new software investments, to ensure the policies are still relevant and beneficial. The Criteria and Weighting Model described in SSP can then be designed to reflect genuine business needs rather than just preservation of the status quo.

The relationship between a software selection exercise and existing policies and procedures should be reviewed, to identify any areas of policy or procedure that are no longer appropriate. Moving with the times, making improvements and learning from mistakes are the keys to long-term business survival.

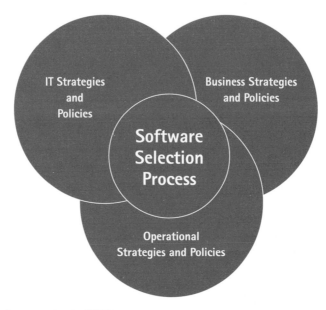

Figure 1.3 – The business context of SSP

1.4.4 Tailoring and scalability

SSP is a generic process, designed to be used in any organisation, whatever the type of software being selected. SSP contains a set of concepts and approaches which form the backbone of any software selection exercise, whatever the size and scope. However, the way in which this process will be applied in each case will vary considerably.

Tailoring and scaling of SSP to suit individual local needs is essential. Failure to tailor may lead to bureaucracy, and will certainly fail to identify the full set of benefits desired from the software.

> The value of SSP is its clarity and focus, not the paperwork. You only need to do enough paperwork for consistency, communication and to meet any audit requirements.

A key question to be resolved on a case-by-case basis is to what extent SSP applies. Fast-tracking through some parts of SSP is possible, though at the risk of causing problems with stakeholder dissatisfaction, lost benefits and lack of an audit trail.

Recommendation

Don't fast-track SSP for important software with significant business benefits.

Different working cultures will also have different ways of implementing SSP guidance. Remember that the value is in the thinking, not the formality or paperwork.

1.5   Encouraging objective decisions

Benefits from new software will be maximised if decisions are made in an objective way, irrespective of the size and value of the procurement. The larger the software selection exercise, or the more highly customised the software, the greater the benefit from the rational controls and processes defined within SSP.

If there are many factors impacting which software to select, objectivity is needed to compare different opinions and features. Objectivity is provided by basing decisions on the Business Case, and building a Criteria and Weighting Model that is weighted according to business needs.

A key element of SSP, which fosters objective decision-making, is the Business Case, the format and scope of which must be tailored to suit local needs. The purpose of the Business Case is to capture summaries of:

- why the software is needed
- the value and timing of benefits from using the software
- the costs and timescales involved
- alternatives and key risks
- the consequences of not proceeding.

This information is used to help decide whether the intended software is actually beneficial or not. Many new software applications have failed because they were perceived to be beneficial from one aspect, yet failed to be beneficial overall.

Smaller selection exercises with lower costs and fewer benefits may only need a lightweight Business Case. Larger levels of expenditure are likely to require much more formal justification and financial analysis.

In all cases, it is important to identify:

- what business process must be followed for this level of expenditure
- who the stakeholders are
- what factors must be included in the Business Case
- what level of investment appraisal is required.

> Two organisations each had a Business Case that justified expenditure of £100k. One Business Case was a 30-page document, the other was three slides in a presentation. Both organisations were happy with the volume of information and level of detail provided.

The Criteria and Weighting Model built within SSP takes account of the importance of individual software functions, operational and commercial constraints and any other key factors. It is used to provide a rational and rounded analysis of how beneficial various software products would be, thereby allowing objective decisions to be made.

The Criteria and Weighting Model will not in itself answer all the questions about what is the best software for an organisation, but it will provide a consistent approach and a set of facts on which management judgements and decisions can be based.

> The Criteria and Weighting Model is a way to score a wide range of factors against their relative importance to the business.

The Criteria and Weighting Model can be scaled to account for the breadth and depth of the decision-making criteria required. In smaller selection exercises that involve few stakeholder groups it can be fast-tracked. In contrast, where there are diverse stakeholder groups, or there is little natural consensus, the Criteria and Weighting Model technique gives a consistent approach to evaluating what criteria are important to the business, and should be applied more formally and extensively.

1.5.1 People as decision-makers

The principles for organisation of people laid down in SSP can also be tailored and scaled.

The guidance in SSP on roles and responsibilities aims to:

- define clear roles and responsibilities
- ensure managerial and specialist stakeholders have a voice
- define a representative and empowered decision-making group
- give focus to day-to-day control and governance.

The principles of clarity and communication apply to all sizes of software selection exercise. Larger exercises will require more full-time or dedicated roles, and need to be more formal in their communication and control mechanisms. This is especially true of geographically dispersed organisations, where greater effort is required to achieve consistent governance and clarity of focus.

> The more geographically dispersed the affected parties, the more formal the software selection should be.

SSP is temporary, in that it only exists for the purpose of selecting the software and seeing it through to initial live usage. Any organisational roles that are set up during the process only exist for the purpose of SSP, and can be disbanded afterwards.

1.5.2 Risk assessment

Risk management can involve the apportionment of risk between the organisation and the supplier. This is particularly true where the software is bespoke or assembled from more than one product. Here the supplier can be made to undertake, for example, risks regarding integration and delivery timetables, or performance and availability of the software, through a contract.

The Office of Government Commerce (OGC) published a guide to best practice in the management of risk in 2002. The guide, called *Management of Risk: Guidance for Practitioners* (M_o_R), describes best practice in line with the Turnbull Report and other corporate guidelines. M_o_R lays out an approach to risk management that integrates all the different parts of a business. All software procurement and software choices should be made in line with this approach.

In the context of SSP, risk management should give high priority to potential reduction in the benefits the new software is expected to bring. If benefits are to be maximised, the risks must be understood and controlled.

> Following the Turnbull Report, best practice is for major software purchases to be subject to risk assessment at corporate, programme, project and operational level.

The purchase of a new piece of software may introduce new risks to an organisation or may affect existing risks. It is therefore prudent to consider the implications of any new software against existing risk management procedures and ongoing risk management actions. New software that destabilises normal business processes will not be beneficial.

The art of risk management is to organise people, processes and actions such that:

- enough risk is taken to meet organisational needs and timescales
- unacceptable risk is avoided or mitigated.

2

AN OVERVIEW OF THE SOFTWARE SELECTION PROCESS

2.1 Sixty second guide to the Software Selection Process

This section provides a radically boiled-down summary of the Software Selection Process (SSP). This will help the reader gain an overview of what SSP is and is not. For further details on any aspect of SSP see the appropriate chapters.

The most important ideas involved in SSP are as follows:

- Define what success looks like, in terms of:
  - doing the right thing for the business (Business Case)
  - value for money
  - how things will be better (benefits)
  - functional requirements.
- Involve *all* the right people as:
  - Project Board members
  - experts advising on selection of criteria and weightings
  - people to keep informed of progress
  - users.
- Build a set of weighted criteria (Criteria and Weighting Model):
  - define the criteria upon which choices will be made
  - weight each criterion according to its business importance
  - work out where cost/function compromises are possible.
- Decide how to create the desired solution:
  - off-the-shelf
  - customised
  - fully bespoke.
- Provide continuity during implementation:
  - make sure the expected benefits become real
  - learn from the post-implementation review.

> Take a project-based approach to choosing the right software.
>
> Aim for:
>
> - clarity
> - consistency
> - focus.
>
> Use your experience – don't be bureaucratic.

2.2   Key objectives of SSP

The primary objective of SSP is to ensure that software choices are based on rational analysis of business needs. This is done by:

- understanding business drivers
- establishing a Business Case against which decisions are made
- representation of stakeholders at all times
- objective comparison of different options.

SSP follows established good practice for evaluating business options, focusing on business needs and benefits.

> A key objective of SSP is to understand and integrate the needs of different departments, and to take account of any constraints identified.

Many software procurements have gone badly wrong because technical or business process constraints were not adequately considered prior to purchase. SSP addresses this failing by giving all stakeholders a voice, and placing the most important and relevant factors at the heart of the decision-making process.

2.3   Structure of SSP

The four major processes of SSP are summarised in Figure 2.1. Full process details are given in Chapters 3–7.

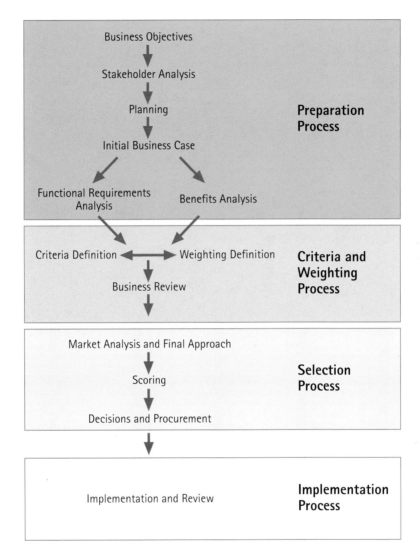

Figure 2.1 – Software Selection Process Model

2.3.1 First process – Preparation

Essential groundwork to prepare for SSP will include identifying the relevant people, key business objectives, and requirements.

- **Business Objectives**
  Clarity of what the business is trying to achieve, and how the software fits into the bigger picture.

- **Stakeholder Analysis**

  Clarity of who would be affected by the new software, and how their voice will be heard in the decision-making.

- **Planning**

  Making a plan for who will do what, when, where and why during the rest of the software selection and implementation. Complex software selection exercises can require considerable effort and investment, excluding costs of the actual software.

- **Initial Business Case**

  An early analysis of the objective and subjective reasons for procuring the software, including anticipated lifetime costs and benefits from its use. This analysis will be refined later in SSP as more information becomes available.

- **Functional Requirements Analysis**

  Clarity of what software functions and features are required by different groups of people.

- **Benefits Analysis**

  Clarity of how the organisation will benefit from different features of the new software, so that priorities can be set and compromises made objectively.

2.3.2 Second process – Criteria and Weighting

This process covers agreeing what factors will be taken into account when evaluating different software options, and how important each factor is in business terms.

- **Criteria Definition**

  Takes input from affected people to build a list of criteria used to evaluate different software options.

- **Weighting Definition**

  Prioritisation of criteria against business benefits so that rational, business-centric choices can be made.

- **Business Review**

  Review of the criteria and their relative priorities to ensure that the Criteria and Weighting Model is sensible overall.

2.3.3 Third process – Selection

The Selection Process involves the identification of potential software solutions, decisions on whether to make, buy off-the-shelf or modify, selection of the optimum solution and actual procurement.

- **Market Analysis and Final Approach**

  Building clarity on what products, suppliers and integration services are active in the market place, and deciding how to create a solution in terms of off-the-shelf, customised or bespoke development.

- **Scoring**

  Evaluation of how well different software options meet the business needs.

- **Decisions and Procurement**

  Final decision-making based on the updated Business Case and the results of scoring.

  Purchasing and contracts with the chosen supplier(s).

2.3.4 Fourth process – Implementation

The Implementation Process involves monitoring any development and implementation to ensure that expected benefits are becoming reality, followed by review of actual benefits achieved some time after a period of use.

- **Implementation and Review**

  Tracking of feedback and benefits to ensure Business Case is coming true, and taking corrective action as necessary.

  Review of benefits and learning points after a period of use.

  Lessons to be learned for the future.

2.4 Summary

SSP is a set of steps and techniques for objective evaluation of different software solutions.

All steps and techniques in SSP are established, good working practices, and should be used to some extent in all cases. However, they *must* be tailored and scaled as appropriate to avoid bureaucracy and allow flexibility.

SSP works by defining a Criteria and Weighting Model that lists:

- the factors to be taken into account
- their relative importance to the business
- how different options score against the criteria.

> The software solution that scores the most points in the Criteria and Weighting Model is the optimum choice for the business.

SSP also tracks any development and implementation work, to ensure original expectations become reality, and to identify when corrective actions need to take place. A post-implementation review is undertaken after a period of use.

People involved in software selection should consider to what extent each of the described steps applies, rather than avoiding a step completely. Failure to do this may waste resources, and could damage the personal reputations of key participants if subsequent implementation goes badly.

3
THE PREPARATION PROCESS

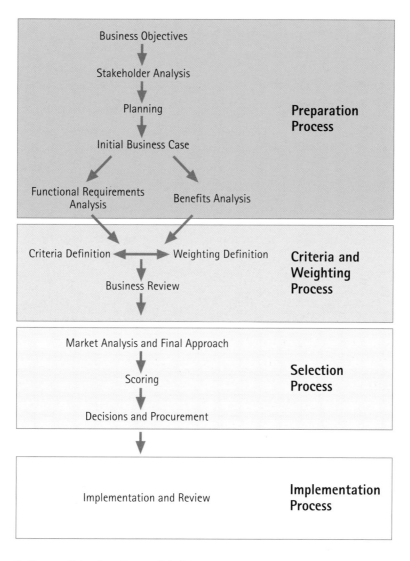

Figure 3.1 – Software Selection Process Model

3.1 Key concepts

The Preparation Process is an essential prerequisite to successful software selection. It is a pre-selection process designed to put in place key structures that set up future control, communication and business-based decisions.

It is assumed that the need for a software selection exercise is recognised by the business, and that high-level expectations and stakeholders are already identified.

The Preparation Process focuses on the following areas:

- Identifying the objectives that the host organisation is trying to achieve.

- Discovering which stakeholders exist, establishing their needs and ensuring representation at management, day-to-day decision-making, procurement team and specialist levels.

- Planning of the remainder of the software selection work where the size and complexity of the software selection exercise justifies a formal plan.

- Setting up (where justified) a small team to lead the software selection exercise, integrating project control principles and ongoing line management.

- Analysing what factors need to be built into a Business Case, and generating one that meets the needs of all relevant stakeholders. This includes analysis of key risks and early views on what form the software solution might take.

- Identification of the detailed operational, functional and technical requirements which the new software must meet.

- Identification and agreement of the benefits which the new software is expected to achieve once it is taken into live usage.

Table 3.1 – Key deliverables of the Preparation Process

Deliverables	Description	Usage
Statement of objectives	An agreed high-level statement of what the software should achieve for the business.	Alignment of views around a common cause; setting of priorities against other work.
Stakeholder Analysis	An understanding of who needs to be involved in the software selection exercise, including process and technical experts as well as business managers.	Effective communications; involvement of the right people; differentiation between key players and onlookers.

Deliverables	Description	Usage
Organisation Structure	Agreed roles and responsibilities for the people involved in building and scoring the Criteria and Weighting Model.	Clarity of focus, leadership and delegation. Gives technical and operational specialists a voice in business decisions.
Initial Business Case	A statement of the objective and subjective business reasons for procuring the software, key risks, early views on expected lifetime costs and benefits from its use.	Used as the basis for all decision-making. Allows objective assessment of cost versus benefits and value for money. Gets updated throughout SSP as new information becomes available.
Benefit profiles	Agreed definitions of benefits, how they will be measured, and who is responsible for fostering them.	Defining, agreeing and tracking the benefits sought; comparing expectations with actual events.
Requirements specification	An agreed high-level specification for the functions, features and operational characteristics required from the software.	Precursor to building the detailed Criteria and Weighting Model against which different software products will be evaluated.
Software selection plan	Activities, costs, key decision-points.	Provides visibility of the work and costs involved in a large software selection exercise.
People in roles	People understanding and accepting their role in the software selection exercise.	Getting commitment from people, whilst still allowing them to continue with other work.

3.2   Preparation 1 – Business Objectives

3.2.1   What are we trying to achieve?

Before proceeding with a major software selection exercise, an organisation should have a very clear view of what it is trying to achieve. This is essential to ensure that any software procured meets organisational needs, and is not purchased simply because it exists.

It is important to have a clear view of how the proposed software will contribute to achieving higher-level objectives. New software frequently enables a step change improvement in business performance, allowing new markets to be serviced, or making difficult manual processes automatic. Ongoing incremental change can make valuable improvements to business processes. However, there comes a point when radical step change is necessary to improve things further.

Failing to link the software purchase to Business Objectives leads to:

- people not using the new software

- large expenditure with little benefit

- failing business processes

- criticism and set-backs to personal reputations of key participants.

> Knowing what the organisation expects from people and processes is an essential prerequisite to making sensible decisions on behalf of the organisation. If you don't know where you're going, you won't end up where you want to be.

If there is a strong consensus on what the new software is intended to achieve, the Preparation 1 process can be fast-tracked. However, it is always prudent to double check that the underlying objectives are genuinely understood and also appropriate.

Having a clear strategy for the organisation is one of the cornerstones for achieving long term success. This is true whether working in the public or private sector. Software can be a major contribution to achieving success and bringing strategy to good tactical effect (see Figure 3.2). Departmental plans and targets may be totally dependent on new software. Therefore, the strategy of the business is very closely related to the procurement of the right software.

Before judgements can be made about what is the best software, the key drivers and Business Objectives must be clear. Attempting to decide upon an approach, or develop a Criteria and Weighting Model before Business Objectives are defined, is likely to lead to implementation problems and loss of benefit later. Similarly, implementing new technical features without clearly defined organisational objectives is unlikely to maximise benefits and provide adequate justification against cost.

Knowing the organisational objectives for the software will also ensure that the best approach is taken to delivering the functionality required. Different objectives can lead to different approaches and solutions. It may be necessary to undertake some business process reviews to streamline operations and maximise the benefits from new software.

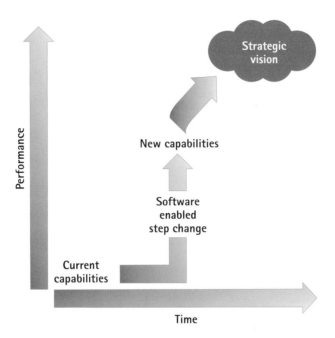

Figure 3.2 – Software as an agent of change

If the objective is to achieve a major internal process change, it may be justified to undergo heavy customisation of an off-the-shelf software tool, or even to invest in a wholly custom-ised application.

On the other hand if the objective is to make small efficiency improvements, there is little justification for heavy customisation; off-the-shelf packages would be a better choice.

Depending on the scale and potential benefit from the new software, good starting points for identifying objectives are listed below and shown in Figure 3.3:

- mission statements
- core value statements
- key business drivers
- departmental plans
- service level agreements
- short and medium term plans
- ongoing programmes and projects.

Figure 3.3 – Identifying Business Objectives

Much of this information will be freely available and accessible, and it may not be necessary to do any further clarification work if there is consensus on what has to be achieved. The information gleaned from these sources will be fleshed out and used in both the Business Case and the Criteria and Weighting Model. Overall benefit from new software can only be maximised if decisions are made on the basis of how the outcome will impact on the organisation.

> If there is common agreement that a new sales support system is needed, there is no further benefit in defining why – it would be better to focus effort on defining the features required from a new system. Don't spend so long analysing requirements that no progress is made in meeting them.

Table 3.2 – Key deliverables of Preparation 1 – Business Objectives

Deliverables	Description	Usage
Statement of objectives	An agreed high-level statement of what the software should achieve for the business.	Alignment of people around a common cause. Setting of priorities against other work.

3.3   Preparation 2 – Stakeholder Analysis

3.3.1   Who needs to be involved and why?

In SSP, stakeholders are people who are impacted by selection, procurement or usage of the software. Stakeholders may be important individuals, or various sizes of interest groups. It is impractical to involve more than about five people in decision-making meetings; when larger decision-making bodies are used diaries can easily become more important than the business decisions. SSP defines ways to involve large numbers of stakeholders without losing the ability to make timely decisions. A Stakeholder Analysis should be undertaken to identify what groups exist, how they might be impacted, and what their early views are.

Stakeholders should be represented in the decision-making process, so that a rounded set of factors are included in decisions, and benefits from the software are maximised. Many new software applications fail to deliver expected benefits because particular requirements (or constraints) of stakeholders were not recognised. Representation of stakeholders also reduces alienation and roll-out problems.

> Would you buy a family car without seeking the views of your partner? They may have expectations that are not immediately obvious. Stakeholders may have different expectations of software from the procurement team – if you don't find out stakeholder expectations you are unlikely to understand their requirements or set their expectations at the right level.
>
> Don't assume you know what is important to other people. Always ask them.

In all cases, it is prudent to identify:

- who needs to be consulted
- who needs to be part of the decision-making process
- who will represent large groups of users
- whether sanction is needed from internal or external auditors.

The following user groups are often under-represented in the decision-making process:

- delivery process or technical experts in junior positions
- business process owners and specialists
- end users with infrequent yet critical requirements
- business partners and suppliers
- operational maintenance staff.

Insurance brokers often obtain many quotes online from different insurers. A small change in the insurance company's software might have a big impact on sales through brokers.

In small organisations the key stakeholders may be obvious and very visible. In large organisations it may be necessary to research which groups will be affected by new software, and who the natural representatives are.

3.3.2 Giving people a voice

It is best practice in project management to define clear roles and responsibilities, which foster:

- tactical decisions linked to business drivers
- quicker decision-making at the right level
- empowerment of staff.

Roles and responsibilities should be negotiated and defined in an Organisation Structure (see Figure 3.4). This should be reviewed by appropriate stakeholders. Larger or more geographically dispersed software selection exercises could make effective use of organisation diagrams published on shared systems, such as an intranet.

The following are generic roles that *must* be tailored to fit local needs and to reflect the size of the software procurement exercise. All roles can be split, shared, delegated or combined as necessary. It is unlikely that all roles would be full-time, even in the largest and most complex software procurement exercises. Once roles have been negotiated and agreed, people should be appointed formally if necessary and should commence their duties.

There should be a Project Board to make management-level decisions on behalf of the business, its users and any relevant suppliers. This group should be able to make the final decisions, and will normally hold the budget for any selection costs and customisation work. Public sector organisations should consider using common UK Government terminology such as Senior Responsible Owner and Investment Decision-Maker for members of the Project Board.

Where diverse user communities exist, it may be necessary to invent a forum where all user views are represented. However, only one or two people from this forum will represent all users within the Project Board.

For a small software selection exercise, a single person may well be able to fulfil all Project Board roles. For audit purposes, however, it is prudent to have more than one.

Never have a Project Board of more than five people. Diaries become disproportionately important in the decision-making process.

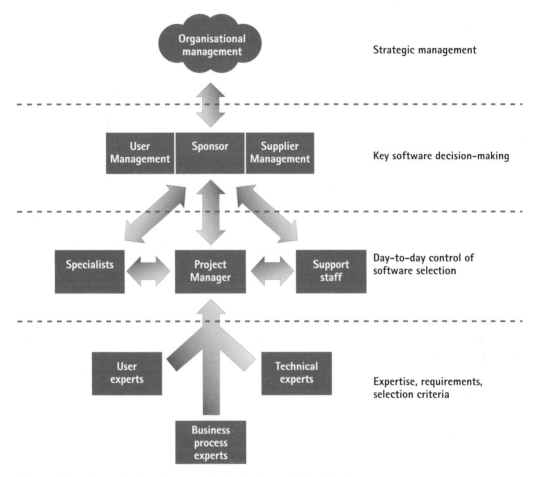

Figure 3.4 – Organisation of people in the Software Selection Process

3.3.2.1 Project Board

The **Project Board** should include representation as follows:

- **Sponsor**
    - A clear owner for the software selection exercise, ultimately accountable and able to make decisions on behalf of the business. Normally owns the Business Case, benefits and budget for the software.

- ■ Matrix organisations may wish to split this role across several people. This can be very successful, as long as there is clear responsibility and prompt decision-making.

- ■ UK public sector organisations often refer to this role as Senior Responsible Owner or Project Executive.

- **User Representative(s)**

  - ■ One or more people who represent the interests of the user communities, and can make decisions about requirements, priorities, testing, ease of use and data.

  - ■ Operational and maintenance staff should be represented as well as business functions.

  - ■ UK public sector organisations often refer to this role as Senior User.

- **Supplier Representative(s)**

  - ■ If extensive customisation of software is expected, suppliers should be represented at Project Board level. Suppliers have a major role in ensuring the software solution is feasible, and that the final solution meets expectations for ease of use and reliability as well as functionality. This is especially important if there are multiple suppliers whose products need to interface with each other, or data suppliers and systems integrators.

  - ■ There may be issues of confidentiality to consider; it may not be appropriate for suppliers to attend all parts of all meetings, e.g. when commercially confidential financial matters are being considered.

  - ■ Other potential Supplier Representatives may come from specialist internal areas, such as procurement and legal experts. Such people can often be considered to be either User or Supplier Representatives. As long as their views are heard within the Project Board there is little to be gained in debating which role they are fulfilling.

  - ■ UK public sector organisations often refer to this role as Senior Supplier.

3.3.2.2 Project Manager

Larger software selection exercises will benefit from having a Project Manager to provide clear day-to-day control. Whether full or part time, this person should report to the Project Board and be responsible for all day-to-day work.

A Project Manager role is justified in larger software selection exercises because:

- they provide a focus to ensure progress is made and difficulties resolved

- without reasonable control there is chaos

- there is a need to coordinate different user groups during development of the requirements and Criteria and Weighting Model

- progress and priorities need to be maintained
- the Project Manager can provide communications and feedback to key stakeholders on behalf of the Project Board.

3.3.2.3 Support staff and specialists

Specialist support staff will be needed in more complex and expensive software procurement exercises, to provide services such as:

- legal, commercial and procurement expertise
- project planning and administration
- technical architectures and design
- business process expertise
- business analysis
- UK public sector organisations often refer to this role as Project Support.

Considerable support is available to public sector organisations from OGC, via IT Infrastructure Library, the Best Practice library, Green Book and the National Audit Office. Much of this advice is public information available to the private sector.

The managers of a privatised industry did not listen to the concerns of infrastructure support staff about technical constraints within a major PC office automation system roll-out.

The main areas of concern were:

- an assumption that all PCs could be upgraded within a single visit
- no allowance for delays caused by bugs and incompatibilities
- the assumption that because data conversion features can be demonstrated they will work for live data without loss of data quality
- lack of testing in key areas of the migration process, especially integration of different suppliers' software on a single PC
- no allowance for unexpected problems because every PC is different.

The roll-out went badly because most of the things they were concerned about went wrong. Users were extremely unhappy about the disruption these problems caused. It was necessary to greatly increase the number of support staff to maintain the pace of roll-out, costs were greatly exceeded and project morale became very low.

The project received very poor reviews and went down in legend as an example of bad practice in software procurement. The personal reputations of the key decision-makers were tarnished.

3.3.2.4 Outsourced IT support

Many larger organisations have outsourced much of their IT expertise to third parties, or have partnerships with suppliers, who may have a pivotal role in the implementation or support of the software, and will need to be kept closely involved. The skill sets of these suppliers may favour particular packages.

Alternatively, if extensive customisation of software is expected, suppliers should be represented at Project Board level. Suppliers have a major role in ensuring the software solution is feasible, and that the final solution meets expectations for ease of use and reliability as well as functionality. This is especially important if there are multiple suppliers whose products need to interface to each other, or data suppliers and systems integrators.

Table 3.3 – Key deliverables of Preparation 2 – Stakeholder Analysis

Deliverables	Description	Usage
Stakeholder Analysis (Only needed in very complex organisations)	An understanding of who will be affected and how they will be represented.	Rounded decision-making. Identifies people to build the Criteria and Weighting Model.
Organisation Structure	Definitions of roles and responsibilities.	To help avoid chaos and to foster timely decision-making by the right people.
People in roles	People accepting and fulfilling their role(s) within the software selection exercise.	Getting buy-in, delegation and making progress.

3.4   Preparation 3 – Planning

3.4.1 Defining and organising activities

A major software selection exercise may be a significant project in its own right, requiring dedicated people and infrastructure. It will be necessary for users and process experts to commit time to developing the Criteria and Weighting Model. The sponsor and other key stakeholders may also require visibility of progress.

Such work will consume resources at the expense of other work and day-to-day duties of staff. Creating a plan for the software selection exercise will reveal the true size of the job and allow rational assessment of priorities.

It is recommended that there be a software selection plan; this may form part of a larger programme plan or change management exercise. The plan should be scaled to fit local needs; however it should contain clear details of:

- key deliverables such as the Criteria and Weighting Model
- key activities and milestones
- natural Project Board decision-points
- costs and resource commitments
- reporting and communication arrangements.

Plans need not be formal, but they must be clear. Smaller software selection exercises will need far less formality than large or geographically diverse ones. It would be beneficial to structure large plans into meaningful management stages, with key decision-points aligned with the breaks between SSP major processes. These natural decision-points will also align with UK public sector Gateway reviews. MSP and PRINCE2 methodologies provide formal guidance on stage selection and management decision-points at all levels.

Larger software selection exercises will benefit from more formal project procedures because of the significant expenditure involved. Smaller software selection exercises may only need checklists rather than formal plans.

Plans, in whatever format, should be agreed with the Project Board, since they will have to fund and resource the software selection work and integrate it with their staff's normal departmental duties.

Table 3.4 – Key deliverables of Preparation 3 – Planning

Deliverables	Description	Usage
Software selection plan	Description of activities, costs, resources, deliverables. How the Criteria and Weighting Model will be built.	Basis for control and organising activities.

3.5   Preparation 4 – Initial Business Case

3.5.1 Is the expenditure justified?

Understanding the expected value of new software to the business is key to rational decision-making. Agreeing a Business Case is an essential prerequisite before staff can evaluate one software solution against another, or prioritise one technical function above another.

> Justifying expenditure on software is not the same as knowing what it would cost.
>
> If the value of using the software is less than its lifetime cost, the organisation would be better off without it.

A Business Case is the set of information used to justify (or not) the expenditure on new software (see Figure 3.5). It is usually a summary document stating the facts about costs, benefits, reasons, options and risks. The investment should only be made if the benefits from using the software exceed the costs and risks.

Many of the perceived benefits of new software will be intangible or difficult to measure, e.g. improved health care or improved staff morale. In such cases there is a danger of wishful thinking rather than real benefit. To help avoid excessive subjectivity it is sensible to measure indicators of the intangible benefit if the benefit itself cannot be easily measured. For instance it is possible to measure staff turnover objectively as one of a number of indicators of staff morale.

A Business Case can also be used to prioritise one change exercise against another, especially if costs or resources are constrained.

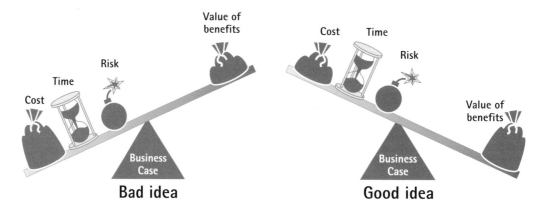

Figure 3.5 – The Business Case

At this early stage of a procurement project it is necessary to get an overview of the high-level requirements and outline costs of further work. These will be refined throughout SSP as more information becomes available. The outline information can be used to focus further efforts and as input to decisions on fast-tracking any parts of SSP which are not thought to be necessary. However, it is prudent to avoid making decisions at this point that can lead to lock-in with a particular supplier or solution later.

There may be pressure from suppliers and potential partners at this point to pre-judge the outcome of further work on a Criteria and Weighting Model. This should be resisted unless there is absolutely no doubt that only one solution exists and that it is appropriate for the business. Failing to develop a Criteria and Weighting Model may weaken bargaining positions and could contravene procurement practices or laws. Expert assistance should be sought if there is any doubt.

> When buying a new car, how much would you spend on air conditioning? €10,000, €1,000, €100 or nothing? It depends on the perceived benefit and funds available – it depends on the Business Case.

The Business Case is a key input to the decision on:

- whether procuring any of the options is justified
- which option is best.

This decision should *not* be based purely on cheapest cost. It should be based on an assessment of what gives the maximum benefit. Benefit is a combination of cost and other forms of value to the enterprise.

A key purpose of the Business Case is to lay out for Project Board members a summary of:

- costs
- benefits
- scores against weighted criteria.

This should enable management decisions to be made on the basis of a rational assessment of the facts. The Business Case contents and level of detail will develop over time from early expectations through to qualified detail.

3.5.2 The contents of a Business Case

The contents of a Business Case will vary from one organisation to another, and probably from one project to another. A Business Case should always be customised to meet local needs at the time.

In general terms, a Business Case should contain:

- the reasons for this software procurement
- a summary of the benefits from use of the new software:
  - tangible, measurable benefits such as lower costs
  - intangible benefits such as brand image

- obvious options and alternative solutions
- costs and timescales:
  - outline costs and timescales should be included
  - more accurate figures can be added later
- investment analysis.

The above information will be used throughout SSP as a basis for decision-making and evaluation of priorities and options. As such, key stakeholders must believe in it.

Further descriptions of the Business Case can be found in the PRINCE2 and MSP methodologies.

> Don't buy software just because it exists. Consider the Business Case first, and only buy it if it is genuinely beneficial to do so.
>
> The Business Case should be reviewed regularly because it will change whenever plans or risks change.

Some of the information in the Business Case will be developed from the business drivers, Requirements Analysis and benefit definition. The Business Case brings this data together in summary format, so that decisions can be made based on summaries of all the relevant facts.

> A significant change to either the Business Case, Business Objectives or benefits is likely to affect the other two.

3.5.3 Key questions that need answers

There are some key questions to be resolved by the Project Board and key stakeholders before a Business Case can be finalised.

- What level of detail is required?

  Some organisations are happy with Business Cases that occupy one presentation slide and a few cells on a spreadsheet. Others require extensive financial analysis and justifying text.

  The Business Case will be refined later in SSP when further details are available. At this early stage, in a procurement exercise, the Business Case should summarise whatever information is available. This should include early views of the likely solution, different options, and, most importantly, the anticipated order of magnitude of costs. This early information is needed to assess whether further investigation is justified. An early version of the Business Case may reveal that the likely costs exceed the likely benefits, in which case further work should stop.

- Is software the only solution?

  The Business Case should include an analysis of alternative solutions to the business problem that the software is aimed to resolve. For instance, it may be possible to make process changes, or multi-skill key people, rather than implementing expensive software engineering solutions.

- What factors should be built into a Business Case?

  The Project Board should make policy decisions on which costs should be factored into a Business Case, and which costs are normal operational ones to be accounted for elsewhere.

  Typical choices are as follows:

  - Should lost staff productivity be considered a cost?
  - Is improved ease of use a benefit, and how should it be measured?
  - Should lifetime maintenance costs be included?
  - Should the Business Case consider lifetime costs and benefits, or a set time such as one year?
  - Who will pay for future upgrades and licence renewals?
  - What pay-back rules must be met for the Business Case to be justified?
  - Is software a capital or revenue expenditure, and what rules should be followed?
  - What form should the investment analysis take – is time-to-profit more important than net return on capital?

> Some organisations accept a five-year pay-back for an investment. Others require a positive financial benefit within a few months.
>
> Financial and procurement experts should be consulted in all large software procurements.

Financial and commercial issues will inevitably be key factors in deciding whether to purchase software, and which of several potential vendors to select.

Expert assistance from financial and procurement experts will be necessary to ensure that appropriate factors and weightings are built into the Criteria and Weighting Model and Business Case.

Cost has always been a factor in the private sector, and is now increasingly important within the public sector. The increasing drive for cost recovery in government and public sector organisations has been added to the already powerful force of value for money. These factors are now extremely important in all software purchases.

> Sensible, common sense management decisions are required on what to include in a Business Case, and whether the Business Case is valid.

Criteria and weightings should cover the entire lifetime of the software product rather than just the initial few months. Vendors may offer a very low initial purchase price and seek to raise prices later, or charge high prices for consultancy and upgrade over the lifetime of the product. All such whole life costs must be understood and factored into the Business Case, otherwise benefits may be negated by unexpected costs.

The cost of maintenance and future releases of the application must be understood, as well as its initial cost. A decision needs to be taken on whether to include costs of future versions in the Business Case for the initial purchase. If so, future versions over a reasonable timescale of three to five years should be factored in. Alternatively, each future release could be viewed as a separate Business Case in its own right.

> The key driver for both public and private sector should be value for money and benefit, rather than cheapest cost. Cheapest is rarely best.
>
> Think very carefully before assuming that bottom-line cost is the most important factor in your business.
>
> Actual cost is, of course, a major consideration, but overall benefit and value are more important.

Pure cost is only the best selection criteria when comparing like with like, as in choosing different sources of an off-the-shelf product. Frequently, there will have to be choices about functionality and business benefit, as well as pure cost.

The key driver for both public and private sector should be value for money and benefit over the life of the software, rather than lowest cost. Cheapest is rarely best. Even with off-the-shelf products, factors such as support, maintenance, availability of consultancy and guarantees should be considered as selection criteria.

3.5.4 Cost of ownership

Cost of purchase is the payment made to procure the software originally. This will be quite different from the total life cost of owning that software over a period of several years. Additional costs, which must be born over the lifetime of a software product, include:

- maintenance and annual licence charges

- operational costs

- lost productivity during user down-time

- future new release costs

- testing future releases

- bug fix costs

- integration work.

Suppliers are often reluctant to commit to future cost levels, partly because it can be difficult to estimate future support requirements. Other future costs will also be unknown; however, they will occur. It is therefore prudent to make provision for future costs in the Business Case, and to address the risk of estimates being inaccurate.

> Software ownership costs may be far greater than the original purchase cost.
>
> Cost of ownership is quite different from cost of purchase. There may be significant further costs incurred during usage of the software over a number of years. Both cost of purchase and cost of ownership should be fully factored into any Business Case for procurement of software.

The vendor may be actively seeking to change their licensing policy, perhaps moving away from site-wide licences towards per seat or shared licensing. Whatever the details are, it is sensible to have these discussions with potential suppliers so that there are no surprises in the future.

It may also be the case that one part of an organisation pays for the initial purchase, and another bears the costs of running and maintaining it. Relevant policies and stakeholders should be consulted.

The cost of any unreliability, in terms of system down-time or unavailability, may need to be factored into the Business Case. As well as any loss of staff productivity, there may also be considerable commercial losses through system down-time, e.g. from websites that are not available and not able to take customer purchases.

3.5.5 Capital replacement cycles

The impact on round-robin capital replacement cycles should also be considered. It may be appropriate to realign expenditure on PC hardware with PC software, so that new software systems can be implemented on new hardware systems.

Alternatively, some organisations prefer to split hardware and software renewal cycles, to minimise the amount of change ongoing at any one time. In either case, the Business Case for major software purchases should look at whole lifecycle costs, plus the impact on other projects such as asset replacement.

Commercial experts should be involved in defining the Business Case structure and content to ensure relevant accounting and legal standards are met.

The following are examples of key statements from Business Cases:

Strong financial benefits
A sales lead tracking system will cost €50k and take two months to implement. If it leads to increased sales of €500k in the first year of operation, it is very financially beneficial.

Strong strategic benefits
A council has to buy new software to implement new government legislation. The software will cost €50k to implement. There is no financial benefit from the new software, other than avoidance of fines for non-compliance.

A weak Business Case
A new payroll application will cost €25k to install, and an additional €5k per annum to maintain. The new software will save €3k per annum in incorrect payments, however there are no other benefits. The lifetime costs of this software would be greater than the benefits; it would not be in the organisation's interests to proceed. Perhaps an easy clerical solution could be found to the problem of incorrect payments.

3.5.6 Different approaches to ownership

The underlying approach to ownership of the software must also be considered.

There will be a direct link between:

- forms of ownership
- the Business Case
- cost of ownership
- operational strengths and weaknesses.

Outright purchase is the most common way to own software; however, alternative approaches are available. Different approaches may have significant benefits to some organisations, so it is worthwhile to consider the impact of different approaches on the Business Case and Criteria and Weighting Model.

Common alternative approaches include:

- private finance (PFI)
- public private partnerships
- leasing
- application service providers (ASPs)
- shared ownership of bespoke software.

Ownership of bespoke software development may include ownership of the intellectual property rights (IPR). Frequently, however, IPR would reside with the developer, with rights of use for the organisation. In some circumstances (e.g. where it may be considered mutually beneficial, or where the software is to be kept from the public domain) it may be important for the organisation to own or share the IPR.

Table 3.5 – Key deliverables of Preparation 4 – Initial Business Case

Deliverables	Description	Usage
Initial Business Case	Summary of the costs, benefits, risks, issues and options. The level of detail will be added to throughout SSP.	Basis for decision-making and prioritisation. If the Business Case is not valid the software purchase should be stopped.

3.6   Preparation 5 – Functional Requirements Analysis

3.6.1   What do we want the software to do?

Preparation 5 – Functional Requirements Analysis runs parallel to *Preparation 6 – Benefits Analysis,* and the two should be considered together (see Figure 3.6). Preparation 5 is an important intermediate step between understanding Business Objectives (Preparation 1) and definition of detailed criteria later in SSP. Preparation 5 focuses on functional requirements; Preparation 6 focuses on understanding the benefit organisations believe they will get from usage of the software functions on a day-to-day basis. Different skill sets may be required, so the processes are separate.

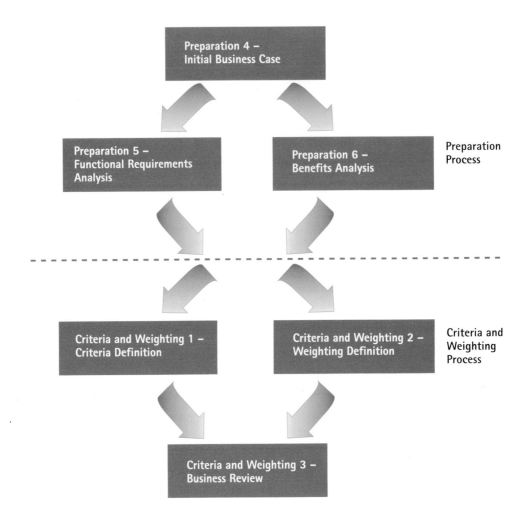

Figure 3.6 – Parallel processes

It is crucial to agree the requirements that the new software must meet, otherwise there is a high risk of failing to meet the needs of some groups. This is particularly important for bespoke or highly customised software where the costs of later changes can be major. Input will need to be taken from all stakeholders identified in the Preparation 1 Process. The requirements for operational support and maintenance should not be forgotten, nor requirements that occur infrequently, for instance annual events.

It is inevitable that different stakeholder groups will assess priorities differently. The Criteria and Weighting Model created later in the SSP caters for this by applying a weighted priority to each selection criterion used. To help manage expectations it is useful to encourage different stakeholder groups to review the whole of the Criteria and Weighting Model; in this way they become aware of the needs of others and their mutual interdependence within the organisation.

Where it is expected that an off-the-shelf package will meet requirements, it can be pointless to generate detailed wish lists of functions; there is no possibility of changing functionality. On the other hand, if customisation is possible through use of a scripting language or after-market services, it can be very useful to focus on defining what customisation requirements there are.

Where bespoke development is envisaged, it is essential to develop detailed definitions of requirements. This may be closely linked to contract negotiations and invitations to tender if the prospective list of suppliers is short.

> What users want and what users need are often different. The Business Case is the basis for differentiating wants from needs.

Many of the detailed selection criteria in the Criteria and Weighting Model will be drawn from the Requirements Analysis. Therefore, it is sensible to maintain the model in a structured form to avoid duplication of effort. The greater the effort in Preparation 5, the easier and quicker building the Criteria and Weighting Model becomes.

Best practice in resolving different perceptions of requirements and priorities is to focus on the benefits that software features can bring. This is further defined in Preparation 6. It is important to focus on the big picture rather than the low-level detail.

> User requirements for reliability must be understood, because:
>
> * different user communities may have different expectations
> * there can be considerable cost variations that result.
>
> Where a software tool or application is fundamental to day-to-day operations, reliability will often have to be much higher than where the software is simply an aid to productivity. It may even be necessary to provide disaster recovery or hot standby systems. Costs may rise exponentially as reliability requirements increase.

Reliability of a service requires more than reliable software. It is also a function of hardware, networking, power supplies and other things. Unreliable software is unlikely to be well received or very effective in organisations and user communities where reliability is important.

Table 3.6 – Key deliverables of Preparation 5 – Functional Requirements Analysis

Deliverables	Description	Usage
Requirements specification	Description of all requirements that the software must meet.	Helps focus minds on what the business must achieve. Major input to the Criteria and Weighting Model.

3.7 Preparation 6 – Benefits Analysis

3.7.1 Why is the software functionality of value?

Preparation 6 – Benefits Analysis runs parallel to *Preparation 5 – Functional Requirements Analysis*, and the two should be considered together. Preparation 6 analyses the improvements that are expected to accrue if a software function is successfully implemented. It is a key step in identifying those software functions that are necessary, and those that are merely desirable.

> Implementation of change should be focused on delivery of benefits, otherwise it is just change for change's sake.

Benefits Analysis is the process of defining benefits that will be achieved if certain software requirements are met. The total value of individual benefits is summarised in the Business Case, and is used to decide whether software is beneficial overall or not. Individual benefits are used to prioritise different features and requirements.

3.7.1.1 Identifying benefits

Initially, the benefits desired may not be entirely clear. Some will be obvious, some can be worked out given thought, and others may take some time to become clear. If the desired benefits are identified and then fostered, new software can be instrumental in moving the organisation forward.

Some benefits will be measurable, frequently in financial terms, such as reduced operating costs. Others, such as improved customer care, are not so easily measured but are equally valid.

Once benefits are understood, it becomes possible to make objective decisions about compromise points. Off-the-shelf software is unlikely to meet all stakeholder requirements, so compromises on functionality may have to be made. If such compromises are based on an understanding of lost business benefits, then the correct compromise decisions will be made.

Stakeholders forming the Project Board must be able and willing to make decisions based on comparison of both objectively measurable and more subjective benefits. It may be necessary to make choices between alternative software solutions that implement different features – an understanding of relative benefits encourages objective and rational choices.

> Benefits must be positively managed from the start if the software is to meet agreed Business Objectives.

3.7.1.2 Benefit management and MSP

Benefits management is a key part of MSP (Managing Successful Programmes). MSP can greatly assist organisations to clarify in the minds of their key stakeholders what the organisation is trying to achieve, and what each individual needs to do in their own area. It is a useful way to approach short-term or annual planning, and can also provide the groundwork for criteria and relative weightings.

The concept of benefits can also be used to help measure the success of software once it has been procured and installed. MSP strongly recommends that benefits should be quantified, insofar as this is possible, whether they are objective or subjective in nature. Having done this, appropriate software can be selected to contribute to achieving these benefits. Over time the benefits can be measured again to prove, verify and ensure that the benefits are actually appearing as expected. This can be an invaluable tool for fine-tuning software roll-out and future purchases, and is also the basis of organisational learning.

3.7.1.3 Features, capabilities and benefits

Software features will create operational capabilities once the software is implemented. Use of that new capability over time will deliver benefits to the organisation. For instance, a new software feature might provide automatic notification of a fault to a central point; this might help create the benefits of improved service levels to customers and better brand image.

Having a new capability does not in itself guarantee extra benefits. Much software is bought because it has many features, yet it fails to deliver significant benefits after implementation because the features do not meet a genuine business need. Understanding the real benefits of a new feature will help eliminate features that add little value, and will encourage more focused (and usually cheaper) bespoke development.

> New features are not necessarily beneficial.
>
> Having 40 cup-holders in your car is not necessarily better than having one per passenger.

3.7.1.4 Benefit groups

For pragmatic reasons, it is sensible to limit the number of separate benefits by grouping them around major operational areas. For instance, software features that together eliminate the need for compensation payments to customers can be grouped together, as could ease-of-use help features. This will facilitate decisions such as whether to select software with better help screens or better control of compensation claims.

> When reviewing expense claims, a charity was amazed to discover how many identical products and services were purchased by staff in different locations. This wasted tens of thousands of pounds per annum in lost bulk-buying discounts.
>
> The charity designed and implemented bespoke software to provide a central expense claim system that gave them the data needed to negotiate large discounts with key suppliers.
>
> The new capability of centralised expense claim tracking led to the major benefit of reduced operational costs.

3.7.1.5 Negative benefits

Negative benefits, i.e. downsides, should also be considered. A new feature may be beneficial to one group but have a big negative impact on another. Decisions should be based on what is best overall for the business.

Examples of negative benefits from new software are:

- increased training costs incurred during introduction of major new software applications
- increased fear of change amongst staff affected by new software.

3.7.1.6 Defining benefits

Each major benefit identified should be documented in a non-bureaucratic yet structured way. Key information to capture is:

- description of the benefit or downside

  e.g. Internet-based quotation software will generate increased sales leads
- how it will be measured

  e.g. the number of leads and sales made following Internet enquiries

  the number of quotations requested by users of our website

- expected values or measures

  e.g. additional ten enquiries per day from the website

  one extra sale per day

- person responsible for the benefit being achieved in reality

  e.g. the person with most to gain from the benefit and who is closely involved in defining the Criteria and Weighting Model.

MSP recommends capture of this information in a set of benefit profiles. Consistent structuring of benefit information makes it easier to track progress toward achievement of benefits both individually and in sets.

Where a benefit cannot be directly measured it is usually possible to measure related key performance indicators (KPIs). For example, staff morale is hard to measure; however, measuring the KPI of staff turnover is easy.

3.7.1.7 Benefits and user viewpoints

A spin-off benefit of defining benefits is that it makes people think about what the new software is really trying to achieve (see Figure 3.7). This can have a very positive knock-on effect into clearer business objectives and better departmental plans.

> If you can't define the benefits a business process delivers, it may not be delivering any.

Tracking of benefits can also greatly help with user management during software procurement and roll-out, because end users of software are frequently in the best place to measure the degree of benefit being achieved from use of that software.

Giving users a voice in the Project Board, plus feedback routes that directly link into benefit measurements, can help break down divisional boundaries and foster the feeling that everybody's voice is valued and heard. If those who are impacted by new software can see a link to business strategy, they are more likely to accept the challenges that the roll-out of new software creates.

Internal user groups, review boards and management reviews can be used to help relate software procurement success to business success, through tracking and management of benefits that the software delivers.

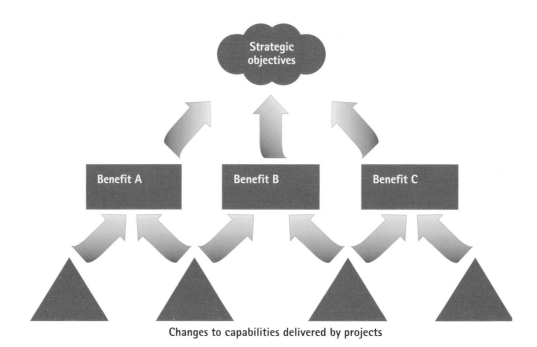

Figure 3.7 – Benefits link projects to strategic objectives

3.7.1.8 Benefit management and risks

A key task of the software selection project management team is the management of risk, in particular the management of any risks to the actual achievement of benefits. Risks that come true are likely to dilute benefits or increase downsides, both of which will undermine the value of the new software to the business. In serious cases the Business Case may be completely undermined unexpectedly.

Part of the Project Board role should be to ensure that the right level of risk is taken in the software selection exercise. In some cases it will be desirable to *increase* the level of risk, for instance, to ensure that project timescales fit a narrow window of opportunity. Accepting increased risk should be accompanied by providing additional management support to ensure the risks do not come true.

Both public and private sector organisations should seek expert advice when taking commercial or legal risks.

Table 3.7 – Key deliverables of Preparation 6 – Benefits Analysis

Deliverables	Description	Usage
Benefit profiles	Descriptions of the benefits that the new software will produce, with measurable values or key performance indicators.	Basis for prioritising functionality, focusing on any customisation work, and managing any downsides caused by the new software. Input into the Business Case for high-level decisions.

4
THE CRITERIA AND WEIGHTING PROCESS

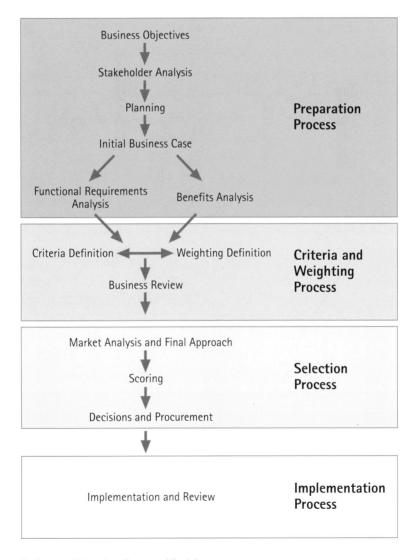

Figure 4.1 – Software Selection Process Model

4.1   Key concepts

The Criteria and Weighting Process follows on from the Preparation Process, which put in place understandings on responsibilities, requirements, benefits and business-based decision-making. The Criteria and Weighting Process builds on this foundation, and creates a set of criteria and weightings that will be used to evaluate different software options.

The primary objectives of the Criteria and Weighting Process are:

- to define criteria used to evaluate different software options

- to agree weightings and relative importance of all criteria

- to review the Criteria and Weighting Model to ensure that it meets business needs overall, is coherent and consistent as a set, and includes all relevant stakeholder views.

The Criteria and Weighting Process is very cross-functional, and demands that effective communication systems be built up between different stakeholder groups and the software selection team.

In large or complex software selection exercises there may be a large number of selection criteria, covering many different functional, technical and operational areas. Identifying these criteria, and then weighting them rationally, can be an extensive piece of work. This is particularly true where it is expected that heavily customised or bespoke software will be used to construct the final outcome.

Where there is already a structured list of selection criteria, the work of building the Criteria and Weighting Model can be fast-tracked. Sometimes it will only be necessary to add business-driven priorities to each criterion stated in the requirements. In contrast, smaller or off-the-shelf software procurements should be able to fast-track this process by concentrating the criteria and weightings on differences between alternative off-the-shelf products rather than de facto standard functionality.

Table 4.1 – Key deliverables of the Criteria and Weighting Process

Deliverables	Description	Usage
Draft Criteria and Weighting Model	Lists of criteria organised by functional or business process area.	Will be used to evaluate whether each software option meets requirements.
Approved Criteria and Weighting Model	A matrix containing criteria and their relative weighting in terms of importance to the business.	Allows rational comparison of different software options weighted against business needs. Basis for stakeholder discussions and agreements.

4.2   Criteria and Weighting 1 – Criteria Definition

4.2.1   Deciding what is important

Criteria and Weighting 1 and Criteria and Weighting 2 are separate because they may involve different skill sets. Criteria and Weighting 1 concentrates on generating lists of criteria, Criteria and Weighting 2 prioritises each criterion against the Business Case. Together, they build the evaluation matrix that will be used to evaluate one software package against another later in SSP. It may be necessary to iteratively add new criteria and weightings.

Criteria will need to be provided by expert users and business process owners from all areas affected by the new software, including users, help desks and IT departments.

Criteria should be chosen which reflect the requirements that the business wants to meet. As such, the criteria may be closely related to any requirements documentation previously created, or may have to be developed through brainstorms and expert opinion.

There may be many hundreds of criteria for major bespoke software, and fewer for off-the-shelf packages. Judgement will have to be used to decide on the level of detail and number of criteria. There is little value in defining hundreds of detailed criteria if there is no prospect of influencing the functionality of an off-the-shelf package. In such cases it would be better to concentrate on fewer criteria targeted to draw out the difference between alternative off-the-shelf solutions.

Criteria are likely to cover the following areas as a minimum:

- business processes and information flows
- data conversion, storage and archive
- communications and integration with other software
- user-driven functions and printing
- help, maintenance and roll-out
- training, support and customisation capabilities
- stability, reliability and service level agreements
- key functions needed to deliver valuable new benefits.

Ways to generate ideas for criteria are:

- functional brainstorms involving key users and process experts
- map current systems and working practices
- consultants, external experts and publicly available product reviews
- suppliers

- trade literature, reviews and marketing materials
- magazine reviews and trade press
- industry bodies and research.

Criteria are likely to be broad-ranging and numerous; larger software selection exercises may generate hundreds of criteria. It is prudent to agree a structure for them that is based on either functional areas or business processes.

> Structuring criteria along the same lines as benefits makes it easier to relate groups of software features to groups of benefits.

Examples of typical criteria are:

- must be able to print on A0 colour plotter
- users must be able to write their own scripted commands and add them to existing menus
- it must be possible to restore an individual data file without restoring the entire back-up.

Good criteria are those that identify whether a specific feature is available in a software package, and how it is presented through user and technical interfaces. The number of criteria required to do this will vary widely from case to case, and there may be very different levels of depth to criteria in different parts of the Criteria and Weighting Model. Where a specific technical feature is essential to the final system, numerous highly specific criteria may be required to establish exactly what different software solutions have to offer.

Bad criteria are those that ask only vague questions or cover generalities. These add little value to the Criteria and Weighting Model, and elicit little information from a supplier. Vague criteria also give suppliers too many opportunities to appear to commit to a piece of functionality that in fact does not exist. A typical example is where suppliers can easily commit to vague functionality; however, during implementation the users realise that the software does not work in an acceptable way. Excessive numbers of vague criteria can lead to excessive numbers and costs of change requests, unexpected expenditure and undermining of the Business Case.

> An organisation considered it essential that passwords on different types of computer were synchronised. They were prepared to pay for extensive customisation of software to make this so.

It is prudent to aim for at least half of the required criteria being quantitative or factual, whilst still recognising that qualitative and judgemental criteria have their place. For instance, it is very difficult (and probably not cost effective) to attempt to define 'ease of use' in quantitative terms. However, it is a very important factor in deciding between two different software options. The objective is to create a Criteria and Weighting Model that provides rational evaluation of different software solutions against another. The danger in allowing more than about half of the criteria to be purely subjective is that little real thought is put into the true value of a criterion.

Where criteria are inherently subjective, for instance where the basic business objective is subjective, like better care in the community or improved education, key performance indicators (KPIs) can be used to set objective criteria as a counterbalance to excess subjective criteria. As an example, better education might be indicated through improved teacher retention rates, and improved care in the community indicated by fewer child abuse cases.

The phrasing of criteria should be checked to ensure that 'yes' answers are beneficial. The Criteria and Weighting Model assumes that 'yes' answers are desirable, and awards high points where they occur. Some questions will have to be rephrased to avoid situations where undesirable features would otherwise score high points.

> **Recommendation**
>
> Phrase criteria carefully.
>
> Avoid questions where undesirable features get a 'yes' answer.
>
> *A badly phrased question:*
> 'Does the software require lots of very expensive training for everybody who uses it?'
>
> *Rephrase to:*
> 'Can the tool be used without training by a typical user?'

Volume 2 of this book provides a fully developed Criteria and Weighting Model for evaluation of software supporting best practice in programme and project management, based on PRINCE2 and MSP.

Consideration should be given to the confidentiality of the Criteria and Weighting Model, and an audit trail of decisions made during its creation. It may be necessary to record an audit trail showing where criteria have come from, who was consulted, and the reasoning behind any decisions made. It may also be necessary to lodge the Criteria and Weighting Model with an independent third party and to keep criteria secret from potential suppliers. This is to provide protection against accusations of changing the procurement criteria after tenders have been received from suppliers. Public sector organisations can obtain advice from the OGC Best Practice Toolkit. Private sector organisations may wish to consult procurement and legal experts.

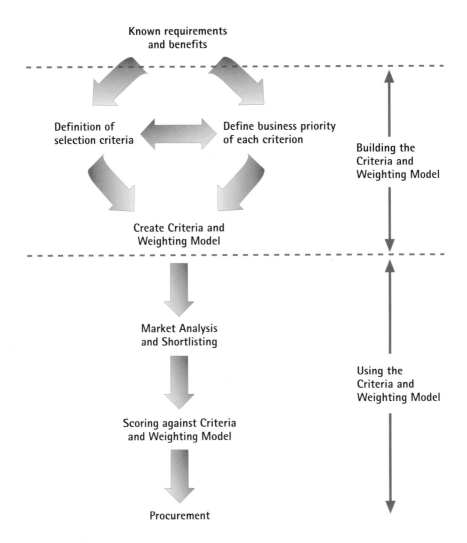

Figure 4.2 – Building and using the Criteria and Weighting Model

4.2.2 Allocate owners for criteria

The owner of a criterion should be the person best placed to monitor and review the criteria and any associated benefits. They would be the key contact person, able to justify, track and advise on the criteria, and responsible for ensuring the criteria are adequately defined. The owner might be a business manager, process expert or technical expert.

The owner of a criterion will often delegate some responsibilities, such as:

- discussion

- research

- early evaluation.

However, they should be prepared to participate in decisions that balance one criterion against another. By implication, they should have line or process responsibilities for the affected areas.

It is likely that there will be more than one person who is very interested in a particular criterion and actively seeking to own it. In such cases it is prudent to ensure that:

- different stakeholders have consistent understanding of what the criterion is about, especially the meaning of key words

- only one person owns a criterion.

Joint ownership leads to duplication of effort and loss of clear responsibility. It is better to split the criterion into two separate criteria and have a separate owner for each, since the requirements of the joint owners are typically different.

Table 4.2 – Key deliverables of Criteria and Weighting 1 – Criteria Definition

Deliverables	Description	Usage
Draft Criteria and Weighting Model	Lists of criteria organised by functional or business process area.	Will be used to evaluate whether each software option meets requirements.

4.3   Criteria and Weighting 2 – Weighting Definition

4.3.1 Which criteria are more important to the business?

This process runs parallel to *Criteria and Weighting 1 – Criteria Definition*, adding weightings to the Criteria and Weighting Model that reflect business priorities. Criteria and Weighting 1 and Criteria and Weighting 2 are separate because they may involve different skill sets. Criteria and Weighting 1 concentrates on generating lists of criteria, Criteria and Weighting 2 prioritises each criteria against the Business Case.

The objective of Criteria and Weighting 2 is to add business-based weightings to each criterion, so that more important criteria have greater influence in the model. Cross-functional agreement to these weightings is important because:

- it avoids excess influence by one group at the expense of others
- it assists buy-in to the process of change
- it leads to a stronger Criteria and Weighting Model
- it helps good communications.

> Many software implementations go badly wrong because dominant decision-makers fail to consider the constraints and requirements of minor stakeholder groups.
>
> Small groups may have very important requirements that strongly influence the software solution. This is especially true if the group provides an expert service, e.g. financial processing.

Software, like IT in general, has limits to its flexibility. Certain rules and ways of working are built into products and it is often impossible for the end users to change them – one must live with any constraints unless major bespoking is justified. Failure to respect what technical and process experts are saying frequently leads to user dissatisfaction during implementation, and subsequent loss of benefit.

> Decision-makers should respect the opinion of technical experts. Most software has constraints on how it can be rolled out and used. If you don't respect these constraints things will go wrong during implementation.

Different groups may have different views on the weighting to be applied to a criterion. There are various solutions to this:

- **Form a consensus**

  Clarify why views are different and form a consensus based on the facts. Sometimes the discussions will reveal that there should be additional criteria defined. This has many advantages in terms of mutual understanding, but may lead to excessive debate unless strong chairmanship is also applied.

- **Averaging**

  Work out the mathematical average of the different suggested weights. This has the advantage of being quick and very rational. However, there is a potential disadvantage of genuinely critical features being downgraded in importance because of disagreements between stakeholder groups. Strong chairmanship and expert opinion may be needed to spot key criteria and support less articulate stakeholders.

- **Peak values**

  Use the highest suggested weight that is justifiable. This approach is easy and quick, but needs moderating to ensure that not all criteria are set with high weights or unreasonable bias.

Forming a consensus is the best approach, provided that any discussions are well chaired and all views heard. A useful technique for processing large numbers of criteria in a reasonable time is to guillotine all discussion on any single criterion after a pre-defined period of time, e.g. two minutes. This encourages clear statements of opinion and fact from participants. Criteria that cannot be agreed within the time can be escalated to higher authority.

If an audit trail is required, all the suggested weightings should be recorded in the Criteria and Weighting Model, as well as the final agreed weight.

The balanced scorecard technique may be of value in identifying criteria that are substantive and of value to the business. The balanced scorecard is based on:

- financial and non-financial measures
- external measures of concern to customers and distant stakeholders
- internal measures focused on business processes
- outcome measures focused on future performance.

4.3.2 Making weightings consistent

The criteria weightings should be agreed in a rational and consistent way. This ensures that the model reflects rounded business priorities rather than any one stakeholder view. This can be achieved through:

- having a consistent weighting scheme
- cross-functional review and appropriate powers of veto.

Table 4.3 shows a suggested, minimalist, weighting system. This simplistic weighting scheme would be perfectly adequate in many situations; however, it could be developed further on a case-by-case basis if a wider range of criteria were needed. Having four levels of weight is a good compromise between:

- consistent views of what each weighting value represents
- speed of allocation of weighting values
- the need to differentiate between essential and non-essential criteria.

Table 4.3 – Suggested weighting scheme

Weighting	Value to the business
4	Mandatory – this criterion must be met
3	Highly desirable – not mandatory but very important
2	Useful – quite important
1	Nice to have

The higher the number of weightings defined, the greater the objectivity of how each one is measured should be. Otherwise, the mathematics within the Criteria and Weighting Model can appear to be very rigorous, yet underneath the valuation of individual criteria is inconsistent. Important criteria may even be undervalued because of opposing views about the difference between individual weighting levels. Nevertheless, high numbers of weightings can work very well where the difference between individual weighting values is already part of normal business processes, provided that there is strong chairmanship to prevent valueless debate.

Using fewer than four weighting values does not draw out those criteria which are more important, and which therefore should get more evaluation in the different software solutions. A weighting system based on two values, e.g. mandatory and desirable, appears clear on the surface but leaves little scope for:

- prioritisation of different business functions
- trade-offs between one benefit and another
- trade-offs between one feature and another.

The 'value' concept could be given more quantitative consistency through relating value to key business parameters such as variation in factory yield, reliability of products or quality of service.

Cross-functional groups should review the criteria and modify them if there is good reason to do so. Normally the 'final' weight should be the highest weight of any expert and experienced group, provided they have reasonable justification.

Strong chairmanship of any brainstorms or reviews is needed, otherwise progress can get bogged down in trivia and cross-functional issues. Useful techniques are to limit discussions to contentious criteria only, and to time-limit discussions on each criterion.

Pass the pen!

Controlling the discussions of excitable stakeholders can be challenging, especially if they tend to interrupt each other all the time. This causes slow progress and dissatisfaction.

A simple technique that usually solves this problem is for the chairperson to set some rules. For example, to rule that nobody may speak:

- for more than one minute at a time
- unless they are holding the chairperson's pen.

This technique encourages clear and rapid point-making, and is surprisingly effective!

It may be necessary to check a user requirement and associated selection criteria against the Business Case and individual benefits. Identifying how the business would gain from a particular function will help identify what its priority should be.

4.3.3 Powers of veto and resolving disagreements

Each criterion 'owner', or their delegated expert, should propose the weighting for each criterion in their area. Other groups should then review these criteria to ensure they are reasonable. Two problems can arise at this point:

- important criteria may have insufficient weight
- excessive weight may be applied to all criteria in one area.

The views of experts from other parts of the business should be respected, provided that there is evidence to justify their opinions. Non-technical users often underestimate technical criteria, and operational staff are justified in adding new criteria or raising the weightings.

Excessive weightings and heated disagreements may require the support of the Project Manager and Project Board to resolve. Since the Project Board should reflect all stakeholder groups, there is a clear escalation route for all parties if disagreements cannot be resolved at lower levels. Similarly, the Project Board is the ultimate arbiter of any dispute about criteria, weightings or whether a veto is reasonable. The individuals concerned should, of course, seek to resolve misunderstandings and disagreements themselves. However, ultimate escalation to the Project Board may be required. In making their decisions the Project Board may wish to consult expert opinion within their own line management areas, and may need to seek advice from higher management within the business.

> Make sure the Criteria and Weighting Model is reviewed and sanity-checked. Common sense must prevail!
>
> A company with a car-parking problem was evaluating potential partner organisations to do some software customisation work. After the initial brainstorm to identify suitable selection criteria, availability of car parking on the partner site came out as the most important factor!

Sometimes a number of different individuals will wish to own an individual criterion; however, this should be avoided. Responsibility should be clearly allocated (and accepted) by one individual, who is then responsible for working with others to form a representative view. If this proves too challenging and there is much arguing over weighting there are two easy solutions:

- split the criterion into several different criteria, each of which is owned by a different person
- get an independent and authoritative person, such as an internal auditor, to decide the weightings.

The objective is to end up with a set of criteria and weightings that reflect:

- functional requirements
- business needs.

4.3.4 Examples of criteria and weightings

Table 4.4 shows some sample criteria and weightings. In a real world example, the criteria should be grouped in a meaningful way because there may be hundreds of them. Grouping by functional area or business process works well. Using a software tool such as a spreadsheet or database is recommended as this enables:

- filtering and sorting
- searching
- automatic maintenance of totals
- report generation
- data import from requirement specifications and other relevant sources
- data export to contracts, reports, newsletters etc.

Table 4.4 – Examples of criteria and weightings

Ref.	Criteria	Weighting	Owner
1	Must be able to read in all existing customer name and address fields without error.	4	Sales Manager
2	Should be able to print 2cm x 4cm address labels on A4 laser printers.	4	Sales Manager
3	Should complete a full back-up of the customer database in less than one hour.	2	IT Manager
4	Menu customisation features should be available to end users.	1	IT Manager

Question: what is more important, one person's special printing requirements, or a hundred people's everyday requirements?

Answer: it depends on the benefits each function provides to the business.

Recommendation

Use Benefits Analysis as a basis for prioritising different software functions.

Table 4.5 – Key deliverables Criteria and Weighting 2 – Weighting Definition

Deliverables	Description	Usage
Proposed Criteria and Weighting Model	Lists of criteria organised by functional or business process area, agreed by stakeholders.	Will receive final review by Project Board, then will be used to evaluate different software options.

4.4   Criteria and Weighting 3 – Business Review

4.4.1 Getting top management support

The time between completion of a proposed Criteria and Weighting Model and commencement of SSP is a natural decision-point for the Project Board to:

- resolve any outstanding disagreements about criteria and weightings
- confirm whether the Business Case for the software is valid
- confirm that the requirements and expected benefits are reasonable and match business needs
- check that the Criteria and Weighting Model covers the right areas, and is not skewed excessively in any one direction
- provide guidance to staff as necessary
- commit resources to perform the remainder of the selection and procurement.

Since the Project Board is structured to reflect the business areas impacted by the new software, and consists of line managers with decision-making responsibility, the Project Board should be able to resolve most issues. There is a clear escalation route through line management to higher authority if it is necessary to:

- clarify policy or higher-level Business Objectives
- resolve cross-divisional conflicts or inconsistencies
- take decisions at a higher level.

Table 4.6 – Key deliverables of Business Review

Deliverables	Description	Usage
Approved Criteria and Weighting Model	Lists of criteria organised by functional or business process area, agreed at management level.	Will be used to evaluate different software options.

5

THE SELECTION PROCESS

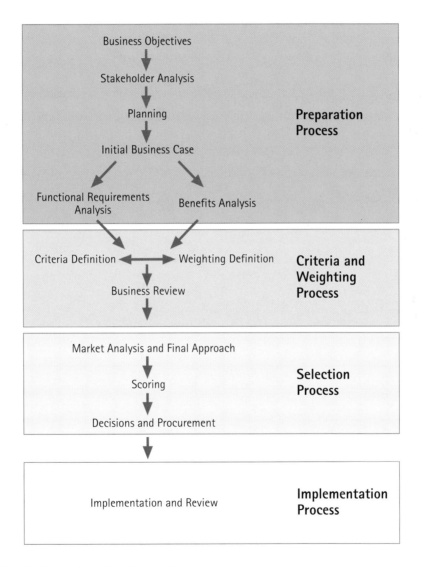

Figure 5.1 – Software Selection Process Model

5.1   Key concepts

The Selection Process follows completion of the Criteria and Weighting Process.

The objectives are:

- **Market Analysis**

  Some Market Analysis will have been done already as part of pre-procurement work during the Preparation Process. This is especially true if software is required to automate a specific business process. The purpose here is to take the analysis further to understand what software products and services exist in the market, or have changed since earlier work was done.

- **Identify any requirements for compromise**

  Market Analysis and increasing product awareness may reveal requirements which are very difficult, or expensive, to satisfy. It is important to review the Business Case in the light of discoveries, and to identify any compromise points in requirements.

- **Agree the approach**

  Understanding what products and services exist will determine how big a gap there is between requirements and standard off-the-shelf software products or services. The approach is a statement of how business needs will be met in terms of:

  - off-the-shelf solutions

  - modified off-the-shelf solutions

  - bespoke development

  - alternatives for procurement and ownership.

  Off-the-shelf procurements are likely to be much cheaper solutions than bespoke software; however, compromises in functionality may be needed. Benefits Analysis and the Criteria and Weighting Model will reveal the optimum solution.

- **Evaluation**

  Scoring a shortlist of software offerings against the Criteria and Weighting Model to identify the most appropriate choice and to understand any shortfall between requirements and capabilities.

- **Procurement**

  Actual procurement and contracts. This is a specialised skill, which is only outlined within SSP because expert advice is already available to public sector organisations via OGC, and is widely available in the private sector.

  Included in SSP are the key points that relate the details of procurement to earlier work on defining requirements and establishing a Criteria and Weighting Model.

- **Risk control**

  A key objective is reduction of the risk that the software may fail to meet user requirements, and cannot be implemented smoothly. An appropriate level of rigour and formality is needed to ensure that:

  - enough forethought is given to selection and procurement
  - the optimum software solution is procured
  - the software can actually be implemented and does actually do the job required.

Table 5.1 – Key deliverables of the Selection Process

Deliverables	Description	Usage
Market report	Knowledge of what products and services exist in the market already.	Prerequisite to finalising the approach and shortlisting of alternative solutions.
Approved Approach	Project Board sanctioned decisions on off-the-shelf, make/buy strategies.	Different approaches lead to fundamental differences in costs and benefits.
Finalised Business Case	Revised and then finalised as more detail becomes known.	If the Business Case is not valid the software selection exercise should not proceed further.
Populated Criteria and Weighting Model	Finished analysis of shortlisted software products, together with scores in the Criteria and Weighting Model.	The software scoring the most points is the optimum software for the business.
Procured software and contracts	Contracts and purchases.	Basis for implementation and any customisation.

5.2   Selection 1 – Market Analysis and Final Approach

5.2.1 What products and services already exist?

It is likely that there will already have been an analysis of what software solutions and providers are available in the market, at broadly what cost, done as part of defining a Business Case and building the Criteria and Weighting Model. If not, Market Analysis should be undertaken now to determine which products and service offerings are likely to meet business needs, and should therefore be evaluated. Early views of the likely cost of the software will need to be confirmed, and this will have a direct link into decision-making about different approaches.

5.2.1.1 Fast-tracking

The more previous work has been done, the more this process can be fast-tracked or even skipped completely. However, be careful not to assume that the only potential solutions are the ones with high-profile marketing. There may be solutions in the market that are not immediately apparent.

5.2.2 Sourcing the market

There is a wide range of sources of information on software products, especially for common business functions. These include:

- information consultancies and research groups (large amounts of information on more popular software products, such as databases, accounts and HR software are available, including comparative reports)
- software catalogues
- internet and trade press
- trade shows
- marketing by software suppliers
- information from system integrators.

It is likely that a range of competing products and services will be identified, including:

- off-the-shelf software applications
- add-ons and third party modules
- development of bespoke services
- hosted application services
- do-it-yourself development tools.

The Project Board should review the available options and decide on the approach required to fulfil the business need. The approach is an agreement on strategy, i.e. will the software be off-the-shelf, or customised, or 100% bespoke? The approach must therefore be developed from a high-level understanding of what can be sourced from the market, its likely cost and functional fit with requirements.

5.2.3 Sourcing options

An approach seeking the perfect solution may not give value for money, because it encourages impractical idealism. Closing the gap between off-the-shelf functionality and meeting every requirement can add hugely to the cost. It is better to know what is out there, then work out whether it is likely to provide the majority of functions required. It may be optimal to have off-the-shelf software that is cheaper but has less functionality.

If no existing products or services are likely to meet requirements, heavily customised or bespoke systems will be required. This type of solution is likely to be much more expensive than packaged software, so decisions need to be made rationally. The Business Case may no longer be valid if the costs have risen substantially above original expectations.

> Bespoke software needs a much stronger Business Case than customisable packages, because it is usually much more expensive.

It may be necessary to revisit requirements in order to move expectations and redesign business processes towards off-the-shelf-solutions. Simplifying functionality, or doing things in a different way, can result in substantial cost savings through reducing customisation and bespoke development, without greatly reducing business benefits.

> **Know your costs and benefits**
>
> 80% of the benefit probably comes from 20% of the functionality.
>
> What benefits are you prepared to compromise on in order to minimise cost?
>
> After developing some bespoke software, an animal feed manufacturer was able to introduce feeds that were mixed to order for individual cows – an innovative added-value service with a very strong Business Case.

5.2.4 Software customisation

It may be possible to extensively customise an off-the-shelf software product by using features already built into computer operating systems or user-programmable application functions. Operating system integration features are getting steadily more sophisticated. Project Board members should not assume that expensive bespoke software is needed in all cases. Although do-it-yourself integration may lack the sophistication of bespoke software, there may be scope for quick wins or reduced functionality at much cheaper cost, especially when combined with rationalised business processes and flexibility of staff.

It is prudent to plan and control any such customisation as there can be considerable additional support costs and risks in the future. If customisation is done in-house there is a very real danger of the software being unsupportable once the authors have moved on. This can mean that enhancements cannot be implemented, bugs cannot be resolved, and in the worst cases application data may even be lost.

Common integration features available in most operating systems and sophisticated applications are:

- hyperlinks
- Internet links and bookmarks
- shared application and data objects
- standardised end user scripting languages.

Many software tools will have these functions built in as generic mechanisms available to all applications. Using these basic building blocks plus user-programmable applications, powerful new functions can be created.

> A company wanted software to help their staff create PRINCE2 'Product Breakdown Structures' and 'Product Descriptions'. They were unable to find any software off-the-shelf that met their needs, and the costs of fully bespoke software were prohibitive, so they wrote their own.
>
> They used industry standard PC operating system features, and the user-programmable language bundled with their office automation suite.
>
> After analysis of the costs and benefits of the different options, they decided on a software solution with reduced functionality but lots of benefits and quick wins.
>
> The result was a highly effective, flexible solution that met many of their needs and was relatively cheap and quick to create.

Many applications now include powerful user-programmable features within their standard functionality. In many cases, what users can do manually the software can be easily programmed to do automatically. This can be used to access most, if not all, of the application's in-built functions, and link them together in new ways with new menu items. Value can be added in areas such as:

- data conversion
- validation of input
- integration of data with other applications.

This is a very powerful feature indeed, and may be extremely important within the overall set of weighting criteria. An important area of value is the ability to automate aspects of business processes and trap errors in data early, thereby releasing staff to add more value elsewhere.

Most user-programmable application features are relatively easy to use, and there may be functions within the application to record user actions without having to write programming statements. It is therefore important to consider what functionality is required of the tool before making final selection of a new piece of software.

If application extensions based on user-programmable features are an important requirement, there are some key areas to be considered:

- they must provide the functionality needed
- performance must be adequate – user-programmable features are usually much slower to execute than bespoke code.

5.2.5 Sourcing and risks

The impact of different solutions on risks should not be forgotten. Different approaches and solutions will raise different risks. The Project Board should be made aware of any key risks, especially commercial, legal and important technical risks.

Table 5.2 – Key deliverables of Selection 1 – Market Analysis and Final Approach

Deliverables	Description	Usage
Market information	Knowledge of what products and services exist in the market already.	Prerequisite to finalising the approach and shortlisting of alternative solutions.
Approved approach	Project Board sanctioned decisions on off-the-shelf, make/buy strategies.	Different approaches lead to fundamental differences in costs and benefits.

5.3   Selection 2 – Scoring

5.3.1 Rational selection of the optimum solution

Once the Project Board has agreed the approach it should be straightforward to select which software products or service providers to shortlist for evaluation. Commercial and procurement experts should be consulted to ensure that any constraints, international agreements such as OJEC, EU and GATT trading rules and audit requirements are taken into account. Public sector organisations should seek advice from OGC, National Audit Office or other public sector procurement experts.

The Criteria and Weighting Model will work for any number of potential products or suppliers; however, it is pragmatic to limit the number to a shortlist of three to five. Once the shortlist has been nominated, the Criteria and Weighting Model should be populated with scores for each product or service against each of the criteria. This can be a time-consuming process that will have to be repeated for each shortlisted product or supplier.

The raw data on which scores are based may come from many sources:

- product marketing literature
- trade reviews
- demonstrations
- trial usage and evaluation
- product documentation and websites
- expert opinion
- questionnaires to suppliers
- tenders from suppliers.

The last two are particularly recommended, since they allow the supplier to provide correct and up-to-date information, and if the same documentation is sent to several suppliers it allows easy comparison. Proposals and responses to questionnaires, and supplier tenders can provide the basis for a contract.

5.3.2 Awarding points

Points should be awarded in the Criteria and Weighting Model according to how well each product meets each criterion. A suggested point scoring system is shown in Table 5.3.

The suggested points allocation system is a sensible general purpose scoring system that will be adequate in many situations, balancing the need to differentiate between different software solutions without an artificial level of detail. Underlying assumptions are that:

- higher marks are awarded for a criterion being met by standard off-the-shelf function-ality (because this is likely to be cheaper)
- software requiring extensive customisation is less desirable
- no points are awarded for software that does not meet a criterion
- points are gained in a linear way.

Table 5.3 – Suggested points allocation

Points	Reason for award
3	• Standard functionality • 'Yes' to criteria demanding a Yes/No answer
2	Minor customisation needed
1	Major customisation needed
0	• Not possible • Not implemented • 'No' to criteria demanding a Yes/No answer

There is therefore a close link between the wording of criteria and the points that might be scored. Phrasing of criteria must be consistent with the points scoring system.

Alternative scoring schemes could be devised to suit the needs of a particular procurement. These could include the following:

- Wider range of scores, say 1–10 or 0–100. This may be advantageous if there are clear grounds for differentiating a larger number of degrees of fit between each criterion and requirements.

- Logarithmic or rising scales where there are increasing gaps between the points scored for each criterion. This can be advantageous if there is a desire to skew the overall scores towards software solutions that fully meet a few criteria rather than partially meeting many.

- Different scoring systems might be applied to different parts of the Criteria and Weighting Model. For instance, higher 'maximum' points might be awarded for meeting criteria related to important business processes, and lower 'maximum' points for fully meeting less important criteria. Importance might be defined in terms of time, cost, scope, quality and risk, related to the business benefits expected from the new software.

Different stakeholder groups will have different opinions of the score that should be applied to each criterion. The Criteria and Weighting Model can easily be scaled up to capture the views of many different stakeholder groups. An agreed weight should be defined for each criterion. This should be agreed between the stakeholder groups, or if no agreement is possible, escalated to the Project Board.

5.3.3 Calculating total score

The following formula is used to calculate the weighted score for each software product against each criterion:

Weighted score = points for this criterion x weighting for this criterion

E.g. if two points are awarded for a criterion, and the weighting for that criterion is three, the weighted score is six points.

Weighted scores should be totalled for each group of criteria (e.g. functional area) within the criteria and evaluation model, so that comparisons are possible by meaningful business groupings as well as overall. Sensible grouping of criteria around meaningful business or technical areas will also reveal the strengths and weaknesses of different software solutions.

The product or service that achieves the highest overall score in the Criteria and Weighting Model is the optimum one to meet the business needs and functional requirements.

Table 5.4 shows a suggested layout for the Criteria and Weighting Model with input from three key stakeholder groups (A, B and C), evaluating two software products (X and Y).

5.3.4 Handling of costs in SSP

The costs of the different potential software solutions are handled in the following way in SSP:

- **Criteria and Weighting Model**
  This should contain criteria relating to any financial arrangements, presentation of costs, risk factors etc.

- **Business Case**
  The Business Case is the place to put summary costs and options. It should contain a summary of the different software solutions, other options for achieving the same outcome, summary costs, investment analysis, key risks, trade-offs and decisions required. The Business Case should also show the relationship between costs, benefits and the fit against requirements.

5.4 Selection 3 – Decisions and Procurement Process

The objective of this process is:

- finalisation of the Business Case
- final decisions about benefits, approaches and software features
- procure the selected software
- agree contracts for any customisation and tailoring.

Table 5.4 – Example of a Criteria and Weighting Model with scores

Ref	Criterion	Weights				Scores for each software product			
		Group A	Group B	Group C	Agreed weight	X points	X score	Y points	Y score
1	Must be able to read in all existing customer name and address fields without error.	4	3	3	3	3	9	2	6
2	Should be able to print style 1234 address labels on A4 laser printer.	4	2	1	4	2	8	2	8
3	Should complete a full back-up of customer database in less than one hour.	2	2	2	2	2	4	1	2
4	Menu customisation features should be available to end users.	1	2	2	2	0	0	1	2
	Total scores						21		18

Prior to this process, the Criteria and Weighting Model has been populated with weighted criteria, each of which has been scored against different software solutions. The total scores for each software product will now be known, and suppliers will have provided additional information. This data will allow analysis of:

- strengths and weaknesses of each software solution
- balancing of benefits and available software features
- cost benefit analysis of different choices and functional trade-offs.

Once this analysis has been carried out, the Project Manager can bring together all the necessary expertise and data so that the different options and choices can be summarised in the Business Case, and procurement decisions made. A formal tendering process may then be required.

Procurement is a specialist skill. Assistance should be sourced from commercial staff, who should have been identified in *Preparation 2 – Stakeholder Analysis* as significant stakeholders. Considerable expertise concerning OJEC and GATT procurement rules is available to public sector organisations through OGC. Both public and private sector organisations should seek expert advice before letting contracts.

5.4.1 SSP and procurement staff

Populating the Criteria and Weighting Model in the *Selection 2 – Scoring* process offers procurement staff advantages.

- The Criteria and Weighting Model should contain appropriately weighted commercial and procurement selection criteria as well as user functionality and technical features.

- The Criteria and Weighting Model is a rational way to compare different software solutions and providers, even if they have very different offerings.

- The software option scoring the highest points is the most closely matched to business requirements.

- Low scores imply a poor fit between software and business requirements. This may imply either that the software is a poor investment, or that extensive customisation is necessary. In either scenario, the Business Case should be consulted to ensure the investment is sound.

- Shortfalls between the scores of the selected software option, and the most highly weighted criteria, are the basis for a specification of what customisation is needed.

- The Criteria and Weighting Model can provide valuable data for use in contract negotiations.

- The Criteria and Weighting Model is a major contributor to the audit trail of decisions.

Completion of scoring is a natural decision-point for the Project Board. Procurement experts should be involved in decision-making at this time since the business is about to make a major external commitment. Decisions should be taken on:

- whether the investment should proceed or not

- which software option to proceed with

- the degree of customisation and tailoring required.

The Criteria and Weighting Model will reveal those areas where business requirements are weighted highly, and software product scores are low. These are the areas where contracts for customisation are likely to be required.

Other aspects of SSP that can provide input into procurement and contract negotiations are:

- **The Business Case**
  The Business Case summarises why the software (and any customisation) is needed, what benefits it will deliver and any alternative solutions. The Business Case will now have been updated to include summary costs for each option, and pricing structures from potential suppliers. This information can be used to calculate break-even points,

investment returns, and cashflow forecasts. Key risks and issues associated with each option will also be described.

- **Stakeholder Analysis**

  Clear representation of affected people. Useful for knowing who to talk to about functionality and benefits issues.

- **Requirements Analysis**

  Clear statement of what features are required, and how they relate to business imperatives.

- **Benefits Analysis**

  Statements of benefits delivered by software functions, captured in both quantitative and qualitative terms. These can be used to compare procurement and customisation costs against functionality, and thereby identify unjustifiably expensive non-essential features.

- **Criteria and Weighting Model**

  The scores within the Criteria and Weighting Model can be summarised by supplier and section to allow easy comparison against costs. The software solution with the highest points score is the optimum one overall. The raw total points gained by the optimum solution may of course be a low percentage compared to the maximum potentially available. In this case it is questionable whether the procurement should proceed; it might be better to focus on a series of smaller areas of improvement.

The decision on whether to proceed with a software procurement, and if so, which of a shortlist of solutions to choose, is multi-faceted and requires management skill.

The decision should be made by the Project Board, whose membership should be suitably skilled and experienced to take the level of investment decision and risk required. This wisdom should be mixed with various inputs from SSP to form a sensible decision on how (or whether) to proceed. Project Board members may need to call upon specialist support, procurement and business process experts, before they can reach a final decision. Appropriate audit trails should be put in place.

5.4.2 Problem areas where procurement experts can help

Maximising benefit from software is not just a question of selecting the optimum package or supplier. The software must also be acceptable to end users, and must perform as expected. These are high-risk areas with potentially large impacts. Well-written contract terms can greatly help to mitigate the risks.

Package software providers are usually unwilling to negotiate on their standard terms and conditions, which are conventionally strongly biased in their favour. In reality, there is often little that can be done about this. However, if a contract is written for the provision of a service, rather than simply software provision, this will afford better protection.

Below are some common problem areas which greatly reduce benefits from new software, and which can be mitigated through contract terms and conditions:

- **Poor ease of use**

  Ensure user trials are performed, especially for any customised features. Suppliers should allow time for working with users during development work so that requirements and quality are fully defined. Corrective costs for ease of use problems after implementation should be paid by the supplier if they do not do this adequately.

- **Unreliability and excessive downtime**

  Agree acceptable service levels, the most common being for availability and response times. There should be service levels for fixing software defects, with graded responses for different levels of severity, and penalty clauses for slow response.

- **Late delivery**

  The longer the customisation or bespoke development the more the need for interim reviews and interim deliverables. Link approval of deliverables to payment milestones.

- **Changing user requirements**

  Ensure all user change requests are justified by the Business Case after assessment of their impact on plans and benefits. Senior supplier staff, and their technical experts, should be allowed to comment on the feasibility and impact of change requests. If proposed changes are not justified, or not feasible, don't attempt to implement them.

  Consider having a moratorium on changes until after the first version has gone live, thereby bringing in early benefits. Change requests and bug fixes can be developed in parallel with each other and deployed later.

  The process for handling change requests should be clearly defined within contracts, together with any funding arrangements for assessing the potential impact of a change.

- **Alternative solutions**

  Sometimes a business requirement can be met by simple changes to business processes rather than costly software customisation. Make sure any customisation genuinely has a Business Case, and that non-software options have been considered. People are more flexible than software, and usually easier to influence.

- **Consolidating consensus**

  SSP has an underlying theme of building consensus around business needs. Procurement staff can help through focusing on quantitative aspects of lifetime costs and benefits, and by reviewing whether deviation from off-the-shelf packages is genuinely beneficial.

- **Restrictions of use**

  Ownership of software or restrictions on its use can lead to support issues. For example, if a third party is brought in to support the application, or even develop it, this may be breaking the licence agreement.

- **Exit costs**

  One very important factor to verify in any commercial arrangements is the cost of exit and any termination clauses within contracts. The nature and implications of these can be significant criteria in the Criteria and Weighting Model.

  For instance, there may be an additional major payment required in order to terminate a contract early, or there may be an exit payment to be made if software has been leased rather than purchased. The costs and implications of these must be factored into the Business Case and any financial models.

- **Trading and procurement rules**

  The UK has entered into numerous legally binding trading agreements with both the European Union and the wider international community. Procurement experts can help ensure that all GATT, OJEC and other rules are understood, and all potential fines avoided. This is especially important in the public sector.

- **Payment milestones**

  It is prudent to align contractual payment milestones with receipt of key deliverables from suppliers. If these deliverables each have clear acceptance criteria based on those within the Criteria and Weighting Model, there will be a close tie-up between delivery of new capabilities, accrual of new benefits and payment of suppliers.

Make sure there are interim deliverables for users to accept.

Otherwise you can easily believe that development is 90% finished when there is still 50% of the work to do.

Table 5.5 – Key deliverables of Selection 3 – Decisions and Procurement

Deliverables	Description	Usage
Finalised Business Case		
Procured software and contracts	Purchases made, contracts agreed.	Necessary prerequisite to any customisation and all implementations.
Customisation	Bespoke modifications to standard functionality, whether done in-house or outsourced.	Fine-tuning of software prior to live operation.

6
THE IMPLEMENTATION PROCESS

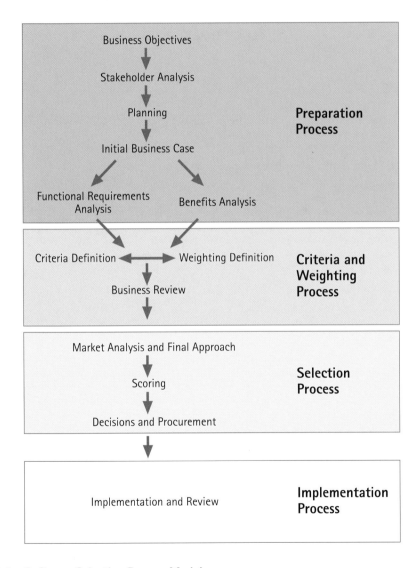

Figure 6.1 – Software Selection Process Model

6.1   Key concepts

Maximising the benefits of software involves:

- selecting the optimum software
- ensuring it is successfully integrated into the business
- learning from experiences.

It is not sufficient to select the right software and then to assume that it will be successful in use. The Implementation Process provides continuity from completed selection through to completed implementation, ensuring that expected benefits are delivered.

Common causes of problems at implementation are:

- lack of user involvement throughout
- users having the wrong expectations
- missing functionality due to incomplete requirements statements
- technical problems
- people-related issues such as resistance to change.

SSP is designed to help avoid these problems through:

- representation of all stakeholders at business and technical levels
- encouragement of communication and involvement, leading to minimum surprises and more complete specifications
- continuity of stakeholder management through requirements, weighting, selection and implementation
- rational and rounded selection criteria
- fostering cross-functional teamwork.

> Maximising benefit from software demands the optimisation of the Selection Process followed by successful implementation.

Key aspects of the Implementation Process are:

- continuity between the selection team and implementers
- review of benefits after a period of use
- capture of learning points.

The details of how the software is implemented will vary from case to case. The Implementation Process provides placeholders where relevant technical and operational detail can be inserted. General principles are:

- ensuring implementation maximises benefits
- ensuring threats to benefits are managed
- ensuring intentions and agreements become reality.

The Implementation Process includes assessment of the actual benefits achieved from live use of the software, compared with the original expectations. It may not be possible to assess whether these benefits have occurred until many months, or even years, after implementation.

Learning points from the whole selection exercise should be captured and disseminated. Analysis of the learning points may reveal that unexpected changes were required to strategies, policies, procedures, operations or cultures; things may have been overlooked or underestimated in earlier parts of SSP. Responsibilities for delivering any changes or further work should be agreed in this process, otherwise there is no learning.

> If there is no intent to learn from learning, then learning is a waste of time.

6.2   Implementation 1 – Implementation and Review

6.2.1 Making sure expected benefits become reality

The primary focus of Implementation and Review is to:

- baseline the current value of benefits
- implement the new software
- ensure users are able and willing to use it
- start achieving real benefits from the new capabilities
- take any corrective action necessary to ensure maximum benefits are achieved in reality.

6.2.2 Baselining benefits

It is important to baseline the value of benefits prior to the implementation of new software, so that:

- initial values and key performance indicators are known
- targets can be set

- ongoing progress towards targets can be measured
- any future deviation from expectations can be addressed.

Establishing baseline values for benefits or key performance indicators may require the setting up of measurement systems or processes. This should be done with as little extra work as possible, since any extra work will dilute the Business Case for the new software. If major effort is required, the costs and impact on business as usual should be factored into the Business Case.

6.2.3 Implementation strategies

The nature of implementation will vary on a case-by-case basis, and may affect either a single computer system or user, or many thousands globally. In all cases the general strategy for implementation should be carefully reviewed by the Project Manager and Project Board, to ensure that:

- quick-win benefits are fostered
- benefits are maximised
- risks are managed appropriately.

Software implementations are often fraught with high-probability, high-impact risks. Senior management often underestimate the risks that the business is exposed to at this time, and in the rush to make progress, inadequate risk management is put in place. The result is often delays, user frustration and technical problems – these lead to loss of benefit overall. The greater the number of people and computer systems involved, the greater this risk.

Choosing the right roll-out strategy is a key way to begin to actively manage the key implementation risks. Two common strategies and their pros and cons are outlined below. Combinations of these two general strategies may be required.

- **Big bang**

  In this implementation strategy large-scale changes are made in a short space of time, frequently with large numbers of users impacted simultaneously. When the new software is hosted on a single computer system, e.g. a mainframe, there is often little choice but to take this approach to implementation.

  Positive aspects of big bang implementations are the short period of change, early arrival of quick-win benefits, and the possibility of step changes in performance. The downsides are that problems can have widespread serious impact, there may be a high peak in technical and user support requirements, and backtracking may not be possible.

  Risk management strategies should focus on advance testing, pilot runs, testing the implementation process, user and technical support.

- **Incremental roll-out**

  This strategy is usually preferred where large numbers of computers, e.g. all the PCs in a company, need to be upgraded with new software. In this strategy target groups of users or computers are implemented in phases against a roll-out plan.

  Positive aspects of incremental roll-outs are:

  - opportunities for quick wins through early roll-out of groups who will benefit greatly
  - the chance to resolve technical glitches with 'friendly' work groups
  - continuity between training courses and live implementation
  - a smoother support profile
  - the ability to accelerate in a controlled way.

  Downsides are:

  - longer total implementation
  - frustration from whoever comes late in the roll-out
  - potential business process inconsistencies between those who have and have not received new software.

  Risk management strategies should focus on prompt resolution of technical problems, managing stakeholder expectations, and the preparation of user communities for change.

6.2.4 Common problems in implementation

Many software procurements run perfectly until implementation starts, then there are huge problems that greatly detract from the expected benefits. Smoothing implementation is therefore an important part of maximising overall benefits from selecting new software.

It is unrealistic to expect software implementations to run perfectly smoothly. To maximise benefits from the new software it is necessary to anticipate problems and be ready to handle them effectively. Likely challenges are:

- technical problems
- steep learning curves
- inappropriate expectations and resistance to change
- excessive workloads due to poor risk management.

Common causes of implementation problems are:

- **Poor control of roll-out**

  The larger or more critical the implementation, the more important it is to gradually accelerate roll-out, rather than going for a 'big bang' approach. Pilot and user testing programmes can be run to prove interfaces and build confidence, followed by a steady increase in the pace of roll-out. It is much easier to resolve a problem with 20 users than with 2,000.

  It is prudent to allow time for testing functionality, user interfaces and the compatibility of different software modules, so that problems can be resolved and implementation procedures fine-tuned.

  Roll-out plans with no contingency after each tranche have a habit of slipping – there is not enough time to help users and the new software to 'bed in' and stabilise. A common solution is to allow an amount of time, say one day per week, as a non-roll-out day, allowing time for consolidation and any recovery work. This is often preferable because it makes it easier to maintain progress against key milestones, rather than having the tail end of the roll-out slipping continuously.

- **Poor communication and users not ready**

  Users and their data must be prepared prior to roll-out. SSP encourages user involvement in decisions, which will help with setting expectations and minimising surprises. User Representatives can act as champions to help prepare user communities for change, especially where they own criteria within the Criteria and Weighting Model, or one of the desired benefits.

- **Fear of change**

  SSP encourages users to participate actively in defining requirements, benefits and selection criteria. Seeking the views and input from stakeholders, combined with effective communication of the reasons and benefits, will help justify change and remove fear.

  If users are convinced of the benefits they will find ways to overcome implementation challenges.

A very articulate user was so negative about a new office automation system that the roll-out was stopped in their workgroup. After the support team spent a few hours with the user, the user realised that the new software included a feature that would solve one of his most frustrating clerical problems.

He then complained about delays in the roll-out!

- **Not listening to feedback**

  The Project Board and Project Manager should set up communication systems and tune into feedback from early users. Benefits should be communicated widely as part of overcoming resistance to change, and problems should be acknowledged and handled promptly.

  Implementation reviews should be held after each tranche of implementation. Lessons should be learned and steps taken to fix problems.

- **Lack of supplier support**

  Procurement contracts should allow for supplier support and defect resolution during implementation. Contracts and budgets should allow for support from suppliers, where their help is required to advise in-house support staff, or to help resolve problems where no party is clearly to blame. Procurement experts should ensure that contracts state what volume of support the supplier is liable to fund, and what the purchaser is willing to pay for, particularly if there is an unexpectedly large support requirement.

  There is a difference between installation of software and trouble-free operation by all users. Responsibilities for the bedding-down work should be clearly laid out in contracts or service level agreements.

- **Change requests**

  There should also be a process for handling the inevitable change requests in a prioritised and timely manner. This should involve representatives from users, suppliers and business interests so that a rounded analysis of whole life impact takes place. Suppliers can reasonably be expected to be paid for their time in assessing the impact of change requests; it is prudent to know what the charges for this service will be.

6.2.5 Learning points

Learning points should be captured centrally and fed back to implementation teams and users promptly. Implementation Processes should be changed as necessary and constantly improved.

Organisational learning points should also be captured centrally and summarised. The Project Board should be active in sharing learning points with other parts of the organisation, and in ensuring that the business addresses any beneficial areas.

Valuable learning points can often be found in reviews of:

- accuracy of estimation techniques

- solutions to particular functional or process problems

- ways to get reluctant stakeholders on board.

6.2.6 Benefit review plan

Few of the expected benefits will be visible on the last day of implementation. Therefore, the Project Manager should organise a post-implementation benefit review, to take place some time later. It may be months or even years before all the benefits of the new software can be measured and reviewed.

A benefit review plan should be created. This can take any appropriate form, however it should include:

- responsibilities
- what should be measured, when, how and by whom
- any outstanding questions or relevant information
- diary entries to encourage the review to happen.

The MSP and PRINCE2 programme and project methodologies describe post-programme benefit reviews and post-project reviews in greater depth.

6.2.7 Post implementation

Benefits from the software should be reviewed after a period of use, and findings fed back into future software procurement exercises. Otherwise, lost benefits may not be noticed, and quick wins for improvement missed.

> A post-implementation review showed that roll-out effort for an office automation system had been underestimated by 50% per user. The amount of user queries received and support required in the first few hours after each PC had been upgraded were seriously underestimated.

A benefit review should be timed to take place as soon as most benefits are visible. This may be as little as a few months, or may have to wait for a full year's trading and financial accounts.

Typically a benefit review should include, within scope, the following items, otherwise adjustments may not be made, and future software selection exercises may miss out on valuable learning points:

- reliability and ease of use
- actual operational and maintenance values
- review original weightings and criteria to see if they were reasonable
- review achievements against Business Case
- learning points and responsibility for handling them.

An organisation that did scientific analysis invited users of a new system to tell each other hot tips about how the new software could be better used. This made a big improvement in enjoyment of the new system, because some of the tips made life easier for a lot of people.

Table 6.1 – Key deliverables of the Implementation Process

Deliverables	Description	Usage
Learning points	Ongoing communication of successes and failures.	Constant improvement.
Benefit review plan	Plan for review of benefits after a period of use.	Learning, accounting, audit, change requests, maximisation of benefits.

7
INTRODUCTION TO KEY CRITERIA AND WEIGHTINGS

7.1 What to consider, and why to use the information

There are many factors to be taken into account when selecting software. The following sections give outline guidance on:

- what the key generic factors are
- how the factors relate to SSP
- how to avoid common problems in new software.

7.1.1 Large software selection exercises

Large software selection exercises should be run as formal projects, and should actively review all factors listed in this book. There may be audit trail requirements because of the size of the software investment, and the size of the potential benefits.

The more geographically dispersed the people affected by new software, the more formal the software selection exercise should be; however, bureaucracy should be avoided. Effective communication and control are essential. Writing things down is a prerequisite to sharing information and effective communications with distant stakeholders.

7.1.2 Small software selection exercises

Small software selection exercises should consider to what extent the factors and processes in SSP apply. Some factors will be very important, others may not be relevant in every case, or could be handled in an informal way. Local decisions will have to be made on which factors are likely to have the biggest impact on business process and benefits.

> A key objective is to capture relevant information from the right people, so that sensible criteria for evaluation are defined and good decisions made.

7.1.3 The structure of factors

The factors to be considered when selecting software are structured as follows:

- strategic factors
- commercial factors
- user factors
- training factors
- data and security factors
- roll-out and run-time factors.

For each factor, the key points are captured in terms of:

- general comments
- suggested additions to key SSP information sets such as:
  - the Business Case
  - the Approach
  - the Criteria and Weighting Model
  - stakeholders
- suggested importance of the factor.

The following sections are not an attempt to list all the factors to be taken into account in any software selection exercise. The focus is on those factors with high importance that also tend to be underestimated in many software procurements. Such factors lead directly to serious dilution of the Business Case and can cause high-profile implementation problems.

8

CRITERIA AND WEIGHTING – STRATEGIC FACTORS

8.1　IT strategies and software

Organisations often have strategic directives and policies that lay down the type of software that must be procured. Frequently, any e-mail or Internet interfaces will have mandated technical characteristics, and this may constrain the approach. If it has been mandated that PRINCE2 shall be the preferred project management approach, then any project management software tool must be compatible with, and promote the use of, PRINCE2.

Similarly, an organisation may have made the strategic decision to use the MSP or MoR methodologies that, like PRINCE2, come from the same Office of Government Commerce Successful Delivery Toolkit. These methodologies are in use not only within the public sector, but also increasingly in the private sector.

Another example is the adoption of the euro as a currency. This has affected many software applications, not just financial ones, and not just within Europe. Any software which uses the new currency or the € symbol will be affected, and there are government and organisational-level policies to support it.

Table 8.1 – Key considerations for IT strategies and software

Importance	High in public sector and large private sector companies.
Business Case	May be strong strategic reasons to invest in new software, e.g. to help encourage PRINCE2 principles.
Approach	Close link between organisational strategy and approaches to meeting requirements.
Stakeholders	Senior management, IT managers, quality managers, ISO9000 owner.
Suggestions for criteria	To what extent must software conform to strategic policies?
	Adhering to the policies and interfacing with the existing IT systems will provide many criteria for the weighting model.

Fully populated Criteria and Weighting Models for software implementing PRINCE2 and MSP are available.

8.2   Financial strategies

Financial concerns are as important in the public as the private sector. As well as the need to recover cost or make profits, there are other financial considerations:

- **Cashflow**

  In large organisations the cost of software may be substantial and require advanced budgetary approval. There will be senior stakeholders to consult and many selection criteria or process constraints to be acknowledged.

  In small organisations all cash payments are likely to be tracked by senior management who will be key stakeholders throughout the selection and procurement.

  Lack of cash may affect the approach, contracts and ownership decisions.

- **Capital versus revenue policy**

  Corporate accounting policies will dictate whether software is capitalised and depreciated, or treated as revenue expenditure. Commercial staff and senior management may lay down selection criteria or company rules to be followed.

- **Financial risks**

  Software may introduce financial risks into the organisation, especially where there are long term commitments, or contract liabilities.

- **Cost minimisation versus service levels**

  Cost minimisation may not provide either value for money or maximum benefit. Minimising expenditure is likely to minimise support services, bug fix turnaround and supplier flexibility. It is important to define the requirements, benefits and selection criteria for the software, and negotiate best value against the Business Case.

- **Partnerships**

  Partnerships, PFI etc. are major strategic and financial commitments that will require senior management decisions. There will be many diverse criteria in selecting a new software development partner or hosted application service.

8.3   Strategic lock-in and Trojan horses

As well as fostering strategic objectives, software selection exercises must also avoid making strategic errors. The bigger and more critical the software, the greater the risks and penalties.

8.3.1   Implications of lock-in

It is in the interests of a supplier to sell software and services that appear to be a short-term commitment, but are actually encouraging the customer to become dependent in the medium term. Costs for consultancy and future upgrades may escalate unreasonably once the customer has become dependent on the new software.

Table 8.2 – Key considerations for financial strategies

Importance	Medium to high in all organisations, especially very small and very large organisations.
Business Case	Partnerships, alternative ownership options.
Approach	Bespoke development and/or hosted application services may greatly influence the approach.
Stakeholders	Senior managers, commercial staff.
Suggestions for criteria	Use of partners/PFI will raise many important criteria.
	For off-the-shelf software, availability of discounts and centralised account management may be very important.

A financial services company engaged a major consultancy group to design and develop software to replace an ageing mainframe. Due to lack of controls at senior management level, the consultancy group designed a 'perfect' system rather than the one that was needed.

The project was axed when most of the budget had been consumed on consultancy fees and expenses.

Specific strategic errors to avoid include:

- Trojan horses
- lock-in
- dependence on external consultants.

Trojan horse software appears attractive in the short term; however, in the medium term it has unpleasant consequences that severely undermine the Business Case or benefits.

In particular, Trojan horse software can have hidden future costs that are not discovered until after a period of use. Typically these costs will be in areas like:

- amount of support needed
- consultancy required due to hidden complexity
- lack of handover from supplier to customer's support staff
- fees for processing change requests
- costs of further services.

These may cause unexpected reduction in the benefit and value of the new software, and may even cause cashflow problems in smaller organisations.

> Watch out for Trojan horse software.
>
> Some suppliers actively try to sell it.

It would be wrong to assume that all suppliers will cynically manipulate a sales situation to achieve lock-in, since many suppliers will proactively work in the interests of a rounded partnership. Having become dependent on the new software, it can be very difficult to change direction quickly. There can be little choice but to pay unexpected charges to the supplier, or to employ additional contract staff.

> A household name company customised an off-the-shelf training course administration system and rolled it out globally. The objective was to make it easier for staff to book onto training.
>
> The old system was not maintained after the new one went live.
>
> Unfortunately, the new system was hard to use unless users knew the location where a course was due to be delivered. Contract staff had to be employed for a year because of a big increase in calls to the Training Help Desk from users needing help to locate courses.

8.3.2 Avoiding lock-in

Causing an internal lock-in can be a significant risk.

Internal decisions can lead to an unhealthy dependence on unsatisfactory services, which it may be difficult to correct. Changing from one major software tool to another is usually going to be difficult; however, if there are major transfer costs or significant lock-ins, the process can be very difficult indeed. Classic areas where self-induced lock-in can occur are:

- using customised hardware and peripherals
- architectural dependencies within data
- non-standard hardware or software interfaces
- non-modular software and communications.

Project Boards should be careful to ensure that software procurement decisions do not lead to future lock-in or loss of flexibility.

It is advisable to talk to other users or user groups and gather track record information on the software, to see if dissatisfaction is common with the supplier's performance, charging or approach to supporting users.

Any decision to diverge away from de facto standards should be thoroughly examined to ensure that long-term business benefits and value are preserved.

Any concerns of experienced technical and business process experts should be listened to and carefully evaluated, lest short-term benefit turns into long-term lock-in or problems that are very hard to resolve.

Table 8.3 – Key considerations to help avoid strategic errors

Importance	High where extensive consultancy skills are used, especially if the host organisation is not expert in the business problem the software is trying to resolve.
Business Case	Use of external consultants is usually an option if the host organisation is very busy. Additional controls should be put in place to ensure costs are matched by deliverable benefits.
Approach	Close link between use of third parties and approach.
Stakeholders	Commercial staff, senior managers, senior users.
	The sponsor should take responsibility for all work done by consultancies, benefits and software selection costs.
	User 'champions' should monitor progress and review designs.
Suggestions for criteria	Are there different tariffs for different grades of staff?
	How are change requests to be handled and costed?
	Are discounts available for volume work by third parties?
	Is easy termination possible without unreasonable penalties in contracts?
	How do periodic review and escalation work in contracts and service level agreements?

8.4 Partnerships

The key point about any long term locked-in relationships with software suppliers or application service providers, is that the partnership should be genuine and beneficial to both parties rather than a lock-in for one and excess profit for the other.

Examples of public sector partnerships are:

- Private Finance Initiative (PFI)
- Public Private Partnerships

In such relationships both parties aim to be fully aware of the commitment being made, and the long-term nature of the relationship is above board and open. Long-term commitments are known, even if actual costs and benefits are ill defined. Ignoring any political arguments, this is a synergistic arrangement.

Strategic public private partnerships can be very effective ways to implement major new software applications or tools. There are frequently financial benefits in terms of minimised short-term cost and reduced capital expenditure, and there can be major long-term benefits through introducing new skills into the organisation provided by partners.

8.4.1 Framework agreements

Where it is expected to have an ongoing relationship with a software partner to provide added-value services and consultancy, it is prudent to form a framework agreement. A typical framework agreement would define outline services, costs and ways of working, so that there are no surprises later.

The worst-case scenario is to be locked into an application or supplier which does not achieve the benefits required in the business, and which cannot be unwound because of legal constraints or excessive termination costs. Purchases of minor software tools or applications are unlikely to suffer in this way; however, complicated systems at the core of a business process can expose this risk, and the risks may be quite considerable.

Table 8.4 – Key considerations when forming partnerships

Importance	High for major public sector procurements.
Business Case	Close links between PFI and long-term benefits.
Approach	Alternatives to PFI and public private partnerships should always be considered.
Stakeholders	Senior managers, commercial experts, lawyers.
Suggestions for criteria	Selection of a PFI partner is likely to be a very major exercise in its own right.
	All aspects of service level, technical and functional capabilities, and attributes of potential partners should be included in the criteria.

8.5   Software and business continuity

One factor to be considered is the potential impact of becoming dependent on a new software tool. If a business process is key to the business, and new software is implemented, then the business can become dependent upon the new software.

The business should consider disaster recovery and business continuity if the software is not available for an extended period of time. It may be necessary to provide additional hardware or back-up services, which can make good any temporary shortfall of service. Alternatively, it may be possible to continue in a manual way. The implications should be considered as the risks and mitigation costs will impact some Business Cases.

> It is better to make software procurement decisions based on rational analysis of the facts, rather than to assume that intuitive feelings are right.

Table 8.5 – Key considerations concerning software dependence and business continuity

Importance	High where there is dependence on software within mission-critical business processes.
Business Case	Should look at risks to the business through dependence on third party products or services.
Stakeholders	If there are big risks to business continuity then senior management should be made aware.
Suggestions for criteria	Is it possible to restore data and applications to a different computer?
	What disaster recovery capabilities and services are available?
	What support services and consultancy are available in the event of a major software problem?

8.6 De facto and international standards

International standards are becoming increasingly important as a software procurement issue. The purpose of many software selection exercises is to identify and procure tools that promote use of an established international standard or methodology. Software may be used to provide information and data, or to encourage certain processes through the use of workflow, standardised templates and computer-based communications.

Integration between software packages is becoming more and more important as the use of software extends outside traditional computer systems into other devices such as personal communicators. Examples are WAP and e-mail on mobile phones, and integration between hand-held devices and corporate office automation systems.

> The importance of existing or emerging standards to the business must be considered before making any software purchase.

Important international standards exist in the areas of:

- networking and telecommunications
- document interchange
- security
- project management
- business specific standards, e.g. for structured medical data.

The important points to consider are which international or de facto standards generate business benefits, and whether any shortlisted software can use those standards effectively. The Criteria and Weighting Model should include key elements of these standards, especially any optional features or parameters.

It is not enough simply to list all the functions and features contained within the standard or methodology. This will generate a complete list; however, it will not bear much relation to business needs, and may well give equal weighting to functions with very different values. It is important to extend the Criteria and Weighting Model, and to set weighting values, which represent genuine business needs and appropriate cultural fit.

Many international standards are complicated, and include many options. It is likely that different software from different vendors will implement the same standard in slightly different ways. It may be necessary to assess one application against another according to a standard set of options.

> The more complicated the international standard, the more technical the criteria should be in the Criteria and Weighting Model, with more weight being given to the technical issues. Expert technical assistance will be required.

In some areas, the issue of international standards is becoming easier. Replacement of the complex OSI and X400 by the Internet technologies based on a simpler common set of building blocks has reduced technical risk in many areas. Nevertheless, it is prudent to understand the technical risks and issues in the area of international standards, to ensure that the factors within the Criteria and Weighting Model are appropriate.

Table 8.6 – Key considerations regarding international standards when procuring software

Importance	High if technical international standards are used, or there is application-to-application communication between different organisations.
Business Case	Adherence to de facto or international standards may be important strategically, and/or bring significant benefits.
	Opportunities for streamlining business processes.
	Adopting complex international standards may constrain future business decisions or introduce new risks.
	Standards are often adopted to force a cultural change.
Stakeholders	Technical experts.
	Human resources managers if there are cultural issues in adoption of standards or ways of working.
Suggestions for criteria	What technical standards must the software conform to?
	Which optional aspects of a technical standard must be implemented?
	Can specific parameters or data fields used by the organisation be supported easily in the new software?
	What criteria will have to be met to interface a business process with other organisations or computers with different hardware architectures?
	Can options be changed?

9
CRITERIA AND WEIGHTING – COMMERCIAL FACTORS

9.1 Operational costs

Operational costs are an important part of owning software, and therefore a key criterion for the Business Case and the Criteria and Weighting Model. The Business Case for most software procurements will include the initial purchase cost; however, many people overlook or underestimate ongoing operational costs.

Areas to consider as factors to be built into the weighting model are:

- staffing requirements

- space, tools and equipment for any extra staff

- availability and cost of support staff

- new training requirements

- extra equipment

- data storage and media

- future support and licensing costs

- other costs of ownership.

A sensible software purchase can be financially undermined if additional staff have to be employed unexpectedly to maintain the software. This is particularly the case if the software proves to be unreliable, or a large amount of user support is required.

It is also prudent to consider the back-up and archiving arrangements for any new software. There may be unexpected consequential costs if the new software cannot be incorporated within existing back-up regimes and shift patterns.

> A company wanted better back-up software for their servers. The new software used a different tape rotation cycle. Extra tapes cost over £50,000 yet only £10,000 had been budgeted.

When considering the purchase of a new piece of software it is prudent to form a clear understanding of how future upgrades will be performed. The actual process of getting a new version of the application or tool onto a user's computer should be considered, especially where sites are geographically dispersed or there are large numbers of people. The work of visiting individual PCs can be extremely labour intensive, especially when they are geographically dispersed, and may in itself provide a strong Business Case for a remote support capability.

Table 9.1 – Key considerations regarding operational costs

Importance	High.
Business Case	Decisions must be made on whether lifetime costs and productivity are factors to be considered.
	Which costs should be included in the Business Case?
	Who will fund the different aspects of the procurement, and how will this happen?
Stakeholders	Senior management.
	Commercial experts.
	Accountants.
Suggestions for criteria	How will future versions be rolled out?
	Can upgrades and bug fixes be done automatically, or without physically visiting the user's computer?
	Are there any additional staff requirements to roll out or maintain the software?
	Can existing staff and skills cope with future versions?
	Is help desk training required?
	Can existing back-up media be used?

9.2 Supplier and product background

Supplier and product background may be a significant factor in a software purchase because:

- suppliers and products may have to come from an approved list
- the size of supplier may be important
- there may be international considerations.

Software purchasers should consider whether the size of supplier is a significant factor for them. Very small software development companies have produced excellent software packages; however, some organisations may have good business reasons not to buy from such small suppliers. For instance, very small software suppliers may not be able to provide the support or geographical range of support that is desired.

Product lifecycles in small companies can be longer due to lack of resources. A new version of the software will usually be accompanied by a rise in sales and a healthy cashflow boost; however, this will tail off after a time. If new development is not timely the company may face cashflow difficulties.

On the other hand, smaller companies are more dependent upon their client relationships than larger companies, and so may be very helpful in terms of customisation or local support.

One aspect of the commercial relationship with a software supplier is the credibility of that supplier, and this may be a major factor to build into the Business Case (as a key risk) and specific factors within the Criteria and Weighting Model.

Relevant stakeholders and commercial experts may wish to undertake some form of vendor or supplier assessment, to ensure that the level of commercial risk being accepted is reasonable. This is particularly important where a longer-term relationship is envisaged between the users and suppliers of the software. This is often the case where the software is highly customised or bespoke.

Exact criteria to be factored into the Criteria and Weighting Model should be defined on a case-by-case basis. In general terms, supplier credibility is likely to break down into the following topic areas:

- existing partnerships and commercial relationships
- market perceptions and brand strength
- experience and track record
- financial stability
- strength and depth of staff
- geographical presence
- ability to ramp up for new work.

9.2.1 Added-value services

One of the factors to be considered when choosing a partner to customise or bespoke software, is whether added-value services such as consultancy are available from that vendor.

If the need for added-value services is considerable, then relevant criteria should have a larger weighting. Detailed criteria must be defined on a case-by-case basis; however, they are likely to cover:

- training
- consultancy
- customisation
- support
- other related goods and services.

9.2.2 Development status

The development status of the software is also a factor. Whether the software is very new or long-established may be a factor when comparing different software solutions. Very new software is likely to be innovative, and may introduce valuable new functions to a business. On the other hand, newer software may well contain bugs, and could be lacking in a richness of functionality that only comes with years of ongoing product development.

> The important point is to consider exactly what is being bought, why, and whether it genuinely meets organisational requirements.

There is no generic problem in buying software from a very small company and it being a very early release, provided that it meets business requirements, and that any associated risks and benefits are understood.

Table 9.2 – Key considerations concerning supplier and product background

Importance	Varies according to dependence on the software and range of services required.
Business Case	The risks of large companies buying mission critical software from very small developers should be considered.
Stakeholders	Commercial experts.
	Risk managers.
Suggestions for criteria	Larger organisations tend to select their suppliers and partners against criteria, as well as the suppliers' products.
	Is the supplier stable financially?
	Does the supplier provide all the necessary added-value services?
	Can the supplier provide the support needed at different locations?
	Is the software free of major defects?
	Are free fixes available?

Are intellectual property rights and source code protected if the supplier were to fail financially?

Is there a software user group operating?

Is there a regular software update and release policy?

9.3   Rights of usage

Intellectual property rights (IPR) are an area that must be considered in all cases. This is particularly important when customisation or bespoke software is being procured.

Expert advice should be sought on the full details of the legal and commercial side of IPR and copyright.

In general the key issues are as follows:

- Who owns the software?
- Who has rights to modify or customise it?
- Who has rights to sell it or use it in other organisations?
- Are there any controls that prevent the software being exported or used globally?

The important point to consider is that there may be very significant additional costs such as additional fees or royalty payments. There may also be legal threats and bad publicity if IPR is abused.

Software agreements will usually define quite closely what 'using' the software means. This has to be examined carefully to see if there is any impact on the way the organisation itself intends to have the software supported or developed further.

Software which has a military purpose, or which might assist criminals and terrorists, is carefully controlled and subject to export restrictions. There are also special licence arrangements for export and use of American software that apply perpetually, and may prevent roll-out to certain countries.

It is therefore important to understand what the business needs from the new software are in terms of ownership and ability to sell on to third parties. Expert advice will be needed to ensure that any corporate or commercial needs are covered in the Business Case and Criteria and Weighting Model.

Many software purchases will be of development tools, such as source code compilers, from which further software applications will be built and then used by third parties. There may be sales to other organisations, or simply sharing of new functions or applications across different parts of the same organisation.

> In all cases, it is necessary to understand the commercial relationships and legal liabilities.
>
> Legal and commercial advice should be taken to ensure that this part of the Criteria and Weighting Model contains the correct criteria for decision-making, and the correct level of weighting.

The country of origin of the software compiler may seek to restrict the export of applications built with that compiler, even though the applications were designed and built in a different country. Historically this has been particularly important where the tool supplier is an American company and the end users are in the Middle East, although since September 11th 2001 the impact has widened.

Similarly, as well as export restrictions, it is prudent to ensure that any further software or functions developed using the tool can be used with full rights by the intended people. It is possible that royalties or other payments might need to be paid to the authors or vendors of the software tool. It is very important that the contract and legal issues in this area be understood as part of the procurement.

9.3.1 Software escrow agreements

Contracts for bespoke software development normally include clauses that allow for source codes to be held 'in escrow' by a third party. Under this arrangement, an independent third party holds the supplier's source code and would only release it to the customer when certain conditions have been met, typically when the supplier ceases to trade. In this way, both supplier rights and customer business continuity are assured.

Whether or not the supplier is willing to enter into such relationships could be significant commercial criteria. It is therefore sensible to involve commercial experts in such software procurement models.

Table 9.3 – Key considerations regarding rights of usage

Importance	High in all cases.
Business Case	IPR and export risks may be big issues.
Approach	Ownership, leasing, rights to use will vary from one approach to another.
Stakeholders	Senior managers.
	Lawyers and commercial people.
	Export agencies, government departments.
Suggestions for criteria	Requirements for IPR and copyright must be clearly stated and checked.
	What export restrictions apply?
	Can the software be used legally in all locations?

10

CRITERIA AND WEIGHTING – USER FACTORS

People using the software, rather than the software itself, will generate most of the benefits. It is therefore absolutely critical that aspects of the human interface should be added to the Criteria and Weighting Model.

10.1 User interfaces

User interfaces usually adhere to de facto standards, with similar look and feel, and standardised navigation features. This is advantageous in that applications conforming to de facto standards can be easy to use and quick to learn. This can overcome fear of change, and can greatly reduce or even eliminate the need for expensive training courses.

> The user interface of software is important because it is so closely linked to ease of use, and therefore achievement of business benefit.

Nevertheless, it is prudent to ensure that the software delivers the functions and benefits required by the business. The Business Case may justify use of a non-standard user interface if there are sufficient benefits.

Most software packages will now allow a high level of screen tailoring or painting so that customisation to local requirements is possible.

It is important to manage the expectations of users, since any new software will inevitably demand changes to their working practices. Users may even be required to do more work than previously.

10.2 Target audience

The needs and abilities of target audiences will vary considerably and it may be the case that the same software needs to satisfy the demands of very different user communities. Dispersed user communities are likely to have different requirements in the areas of:

- language
- terminology

- keyboards
- tools
- ways of working
- cultural differences.

> If software is to be used and easily accepted by users, it must be appropriate for its target audience.

If it is possible to tailor the language and presentation of software, this is a bonus. However, if it is not, it will be essential to decide what is required in the best interests of the business. A typical question might be 'is it best to fulfil the needs of one specialist community such as the scientists, or is it better to have a generally applicable software tool that does not excel in any one area but provides an average solution to most people?'

It is important to understand the needs of all communities, and to represent them in terms of criteria and weightings. This will ensure that needs are understood, and the best thing is done for the business as a whole.

The level of user capability and competence must also be understood and catered for. Expert users may require different functionality from novices. This is a classic case where the ability to add new functions and menu items, and to provide user profiles, can be very valuable to a business.

> The different needs of expert and novice users can be addressed if user profiles and menus can be customised easily.

If a software tool can customise itself according to the log-in name of the user, then this can allow the same tool to be presented in different ways to different users.

There is also a very close link here to security and confidentiality of information, which can be controlled on the basis of the log-in name, provided that the functionality is built into an application. It is therefore important to consider those personalisation and security criteria that must go into the evaluation model.

10.3 Skill and experience required

Another area to be considered when purchasing software tools is the level of skill and experience required to implement, use and support the product.

If the user community is fairly inexperienced, then the software tools should ideally be easy to use, with additional training available as required. This cost should be factored into the Business Case.

If the tool is very complex, or includes specialist jargon, then it is unlikely to be used effectively by inexperienced users without extensive training and support. On the other hand, the same software may be highly effective for technical specialists, or people who are already experts in the subject matter. Many software packages will allow functions to be enabled or disabled on a group or individual basis, thereby allowing a tailored user interface to be presented that meets the needs of each user.

> The moral of the story is to ensure that the needs of the user communities are understood, and that appropriate criteria and weightings are set. This will ensure that users receive software that is valuable, useful, easy to use and effective.

10.4 Language and internationalisation

International organisations are likely to have a number of selection criteria based around language and international issues.

For instance, some user communities in an international company may not wish, or be able, to use English language software. There may be a need for the same functionality to be presented in different languages. Some of this functionality may be provided by the operating system, e.g. in terms of date formats, time zones and currency symbols. However, considerable software development effort is required to make an application fully functional in multiple languages and national styles.

> It is dangerous to assume that applications will be available in multiple languages.

It is prudent to understand the criteria that the software must meet, and to add these to the Criteria and Weighting Model. An international review team may be required to ensure that all such needs are identified.

A second area to consider is the internationalisation features other than the language itself. For instance, date formats vary from country to country and where it is necessary to transfer data and share workspaces, there must be appropriate solutions to issues such as dates.

> Is 12/7 the 12th of July or the 7th of December?

There may also be issues with time zones, keyboard mappings, currency symbols and number formats. Organisations exposed to these issues should create a set of software evaluation criteria and weightings that reflect all requirements.

10.5 User groups and external resources

User groups and external resources can add considerable value to a software purchase, and might be included in the Criteria and Weighting Model.

Availability of active user groups and additional resources such as bulletin boards and newsgroups may be a major differentiating factor between software applications. Active user groups can provide many added-value services, often at modest or zero cost.

Typical user group services include:

- help and advice
- worked examples
- templates
- bug fixes and workarounds
- share and learn opportunities
- representation of user communities to suppliers.

Additionally, growth of the Internet has spawned many websites where valuable information and advice about a particular software package or business problem can be found. These sites and their resources can be very valuable, and are often free.

A software tool or application may be able to interface directly to these Internet-based resources, and this may be an important bonus. One example is drawing packages which have in-built knowledge of free clipart libraries, which are available on the Internet. Vast quantities of clipart can be searched and downloaded relatively quickly and without charge, providing greater diversity and richness of resources than it would be feasible to provide on every desktop locally.

The PRINCE2 User Group is a good example of an active user group, meeting regularly and being active in promoting PRINCE2 as an effective project management methodology. The group meets formally twice a year to discuss different aspects of PRINCE2, to share experiences and consult with experts.

Table 10.1 – Key considerations concerning user groups and external resources

Importance	High, especially in international organisations.
Business Case	Might cross national boundaries.
Stakeholders	Senior managers.
	Users from all the countries and communities affected.
Suggestions for criteria	Is the user interface easy to use?
	Does the software meet the needs of experts and novices?
	Can user profiles be customised?
	Are international issues handled properly?
	What criteria must be met in the area of passing data from one country to another?
	Is there an active user group that provides resources and support?

10.6 Manuals

The quality and availability of manuals and help resources is likely to be a criterion for all but the most trivial of software tools and applications.

In recent years there has been a trend in most PC-based applications towards providing fewer paper-based manuals and more online resources. Overall this is beneficial to IT-literate users, since well-written electronic manuals are easier to search and take up less office space. However, in non-computerised environments it may be beneficial to provide printed manuals. Also, some users may need to consult manuals away from the terminal where they use the software.

Rather than providing electronic manuals within the application, manuals may only be available over the Internet. This can be problematical in some organisations because of security rules, cost and other threats associated with use of the Internet.

The important point is to ensure that there is clear understanding of the requirements of the different user groups, and that criteria and weightings reflect those needs.

One area to verify is that any requirement to copy manuals is met by the licence agreements of the software product. The licence may be violated, and the organisation exposed to legal challenges, if it is assumed that electronic or paper manuals can be copied without further reference to the supplier. There may be an additional cost to pay for each user.

The requirement for manuals may be greater with bespoke software, especially for highly customised technical architectures or capacity models. Such manuals may be an important component of training modules.

Table 10.2 – Key considerations for manuals

Importance	Likely to be very important to some users and not important at all to others.
Business Case	If users cannot use the software the Business Case is undermined.
Stakeholders	Computer users.
	Non IT-literate staff.
	Special interest groups.
	Disabled staff.
Suggestions for criteria	Are manuals available in all the required formats?
	Are the needs of disabled staff met?
	Can the manuals be easily understood by typical users?
	Do the manuals explain the right things?
	Are manuals available in the desired languages?

11
CRITERIA AND WEIGHTING – TRAINING FACTORS

11.1 Availability

Availability of training is an important factor in any software purchase. If users or operators are unable to perform their daily duties using the new software, then it is unlikely to be in regular use and will not achieve the business benefits expected. This will undermine the Business Case and can lead to very severe acceptance problems.

> Availability, scope and quality of training are important considerations, since if a new software application cannot be used, it will not be of much benefit.
>
> Many organisations train their own trainers, who then go on to train the rest of the staff. This can be a highly cost-effective option.

Various aspects of training are important enough to be factored into the Business Case and Criteria and Weighting Model:

- cost
- geographical availability
- number of trainers available
- depth of experience of trainers
- likely success rate of training
- how success will be measured.

11.2 Training hardware requirements

A factor to be checked during the software evaluation exercise is whether any additional training hardware is required, or whether additional training rooms have to be provided. These items may attract considerable cost or cause disruption, which should be factored into the Business Case and form part of the evaluation process.

Unexpected training costs

A company did not spot that additional file server computers would be needed for operator training courses at several different locations. This was over €100k of unbudgeted expense.

During the tendering stage, a government department committed to providing suitable rooms in which to run user training courses. Months later the training courses were ready; however, the rooms were no longer available. The training took place in unsuitable rooms – users found it difficult to learn and this increased resistance to adopting the new software.

11.3 Competition and benefits

If there is competition to provide training, this is likely to be beneficial. A wide variety of training providers can offer diversity in terms of course content and delivery, and also keep training course costs relatively low. During the procurement phase, if bidders are aware that there are other training companies, bids will usually be lower.

However, it is important to bear in mind that cost is not the only criterion in selecting training. The benefits associated with a particular training campaign must also be considered. This factor is closely allied to the different types of training provided by different providers.

If the benefits that the organisation is expecting from its new software are clearly defined, this will help provide the objective basis for deciding which training provider to use.

11.4 Location and frequency

Location and frequency of training courses is an important factor. A small training company may be able to provide a very good price; however, there must be question marks over whether a national roll-out programme is too much for them to take on. On the other hand, a large and more well-established training company may have ample capability to take on a national roll-out programme; however, they may not be particularly cheap.

The size of the training provider is not in itself the most important criterion, since smaller organisations are more likely to be responsive to particular needs, and have everything to gain from being flexible and offering tailored training for different user groups. The most important thing is to select a training provider who can provide sufficient volume of training seats in the right place at the right rate of delivery.

11.5 Trainer skills

The suitability of trainers should also be verified during procurement of a software tool. The best trainers are those who not only know the product they are training on, but have also used the product in a real-world environment. This experience can bring a course to life and build commitment from delegates to implement quick wins in key areas. Look for training companies who can provide a wide range of different trainers with a mix of experience as well as classroom skills.

Different groups of users will require different levels of training and therefore different trainers. For instance, senior managers may have specific aspects of the new software that they wish to explore during a training course. If the trainer is unable to understand the business issues involved, then they are unlikely to provide effective training.

Similarly, the needs of operational staff, particularly for high technology products, will be quite different from those of the end user community. If the trainers have no experience of running an IT system, or of maintaining service delivery quality, then they may not be able to provide the best training for the operational staff.

11.6 Training paths

Different groups will need different training. Training providers should be able to meet the diverse needs, otherwise the software may not be adopted.

If the training requirements are large for many users, the Project Board should verify that the Business Case is realistic. The new software may cause major loss of productivity during training and subsequent learning; this might have to be factored in as a cost or negative benefit in the Business Case.

If the new tool relates to a career skill, such as project management, it may be appropriate for formal examination courses to be available to some groups of staff. Other groups, however, may only be interested in management or technical overview presentations, or some sort of themed workshop for their topic of interest. If there is only one type of training available for a particular software tool, then this raises questions as to the suitability of that tool, and whether the users will be content to use it in practice.

An organisation introduced PCs to the majority of its staff. There was an unexpected reluctance among some staff to use a mouse. Extra support and mouse training had to be provided.

11.7 Training approaches

Availability of different approaches to training is an important criterion.

Traditional classroom training can be very effective, especially if mixed with examples and case studies from a typical user environment. However, classroom-based training can be difficult for some users to attend, due to diary pressures, part-time working and operational commitments. For such users it can be very valuable to find Internet, intranet or portable training solutions.

Online and portable training solutions can be deployed using computer networks, or even used at home in the user's own time. Availability of electronic-based training can be an important factor in software procurement where a user community includes a high proportion of:

- part-time workers
- people with disabilities
- people with severe diary pressures.

11.8 Self-help

Do not assume that external training must accompany any new software purchase. Good quality help and tutorials are often built into an application, and this may be sufficient to meet the needs of the majority of users. This can dramatically reduce the costs of installation and ownership of a software tool.

It is also true that an organisation can create its own help system with relative ease, presenting context-sensitive assistance with de facto industry standard look and feel. It is frequently possible to integrate a home-grown help application into the menus of the new software. Often the software tool or application will contain a user-programmable language or application extension capability, which will allow new items to be added to menus.

Similarly, it should be relatively easy, and therefore cost effective, for a software supplier to customise help pages to the needs of a particular organisation or group.

Any potential licence issues should be investigated and understood before any customisation of a third party product takes place.

Table 11.1 – Key considerations for training and self-help

Importance	Varies according to user needs and size of benefits.
Business Case	Are additional hardware and venue costs catered for?
	Should lost work during training be considered a cost?
Stakeholders	Users.
	Human resources.
Suggestions for criteria	Can training be sourced from more than one provider?
	Is training available at all the locations?
	Can the training provider deliver training at the right rate of delivery?
	Have trainers used the software in the real world?
	Are trainers experienced in the right industry or business processes?
	Is a range of trainers available for different user group requirements?
	Is an appropriate range of courses available?
	Is non-classroom training available?
	Is the built-in help an effective alternative to formal training courses?
	Are there online tutorials in the software?
	Can customised help be added by users?

12
CRITERIA AND WEIGHTING – DATA AND SECURITY FACTORS

12.1 The value of data

The data held within computer systems is one of the greatest assets of most businesses. It is essential to analyse in-depth how existing data will be integrated with the new application, before making any commitments to new software.

> One of the biggest causes of failed software implementations is the inability to handle data in the way the business needs.

The most important factors are:

- access to old formats of data
- ability to translate data from old format to new format without loss of information
- ability to link data together in effective ways.

Access to new data, or innovative ways to integrate data, may be a major benefit.

> **News ways with old data**
>
> If supermarkets can analyse people's spending patterns, they can make personalised special offers.
>
> Banks track the location and nature of credit card transactions as a way to spot fraud.

Data cannot be considered in isolation. Business information flows are essentially to do with moving data from one processing point to the next, adding value in an effective and efficient way. Therefore it is most important that business functions are preserved or improved upon in any new system.

Achieving this in practice is a matter of:

- establishing the facts about requirements and expected benefits
- getting the right people involved

- managing change effectively
- doing what is right for the business rather than individuals.

SSP describes how to do this in terms of the Business Case, benefits, selection criteria and stakeholder representation.

It is also important to consider the impact on data shared with customers and business partners. Even if major benefit is to be generated from a new software application, it will still be necessary to very actively manage change with distant partners, to ensure a smooth transition.

> Changing the format of data is very risky. It can be done, but not necessarily first time and without error.
>
> Handling exceptions can be disproportionately time-consuming, and a business process may have to stop whilst data conversion is ongoing.
>
> Changing the data structure of a military payroll system required two days of system downtime. This caused serious disruption to the payroll processes. During the restructuring it was discovered that nearly 200 people were being paid twice!

12.2 Access to legacy data

Access to legacy data can be achieved in a number of ways, for instance:

- direct access
- conversion
- re-entry.

The three different approaches have different benefits and challenges.

12.2.1 Direct access

Direct access is where the new software reads data from a legacy application or database. The new software must therefore understand the format of the old data, and be able to reproduce its functionality. This can be effective and easy, as, for instance, between major versions of bookkeeping applications.

Much more problematical, and therefore risky, is where one application has to read the data created by another. Such cases rarely provide perfect translation first time, every time.

> A major government body wanted to convert 100% of all its legal documents from a legacy format to the new one, without loss of formatting, and without any re-keying. This was unrealistic and not achievable because of the wide range of formatting used in the past.

Direct data access can be a low-cost solution provided that the new application can read the old format directly and without loss of accuracy. This may well be very cost effective and also efficient; however, there may be serious downsides in terms of preserving old or corrupt data, or preserving old formats that should be replaced. It may be prudent to review data quality so that optimal business decisions can be made.

As well as considering the format of data, it is also necessary to provide access to the legacy databases or files. It may be possible to relocate the legacy data onto a new computer system, if there is a compatible media or network. A much more complicated, and typically more expensive, solution is to provide a gateway between new and legacy systems. Whether implemented in hardware or software, such a gateway is likely to be a considerable cost, which should be factored into the Business Case for the new software application or tool.

12.2.2 Conversion

Data conversion is where data is converted from an old format to the format required by a new software application. The full impact and cost of data conversion must be considered before committing to do it, as it is frequently more troublesome and expensive than expected.

Data conversion from one format to another is rarely 100% successful. There is usually some degree of functionality or information that is lost as part of the conversion process, and the more complex the data the more likely this is to occur. For instance, when converting one document format to another, certain text features, column layouts or styles may not be transferred. Although the plain text may be visible, there may be critical information or graphics that are lost.

> If the data is mainly text-based or not particularly critical, less than perfect conversion may be of no great importance. However, if, for instance, the data is financial pension data, it is critical that the data is transferred without loss of accuracy.

The most critical criterion in the purchase of a new application may be the effectiveness of data conversion from previous systems.

> **Recommendation**
>
> Expert users should undertake detailed trial data conversion, to ensure that there are no surprises in the process.
>
> Correction of errors usually takes far longer than expected.

If automatic data conversion is envisaged, it is important to bear in mind that there will be some records that will need manual intervention. Cost estimates should allow sufficient time and resources for manual correction of non-standard records and errors. This may be a very time-consuming process and may require many staff, who will need space to work, IT systems, etc. The likely costs and effort should be factored into your cost benefit analysis, plus a healthy contingency.

It may be necessary to extract a sub-set from the legacy data. This raises many of the same issues as conversion, plus the need to accurately define and select the data required.

12.2.3 Re-entry

Re-entry of data is where legacy data is entered into the new software, through keying, scanning, re-drawing etc.

Re-entry of data is an option; however, it may be very expensive and prone to inaccuracy depending on the nature and size of the data. Vast amounts of data may have been accumulated over many years of business operation. Frequently it will not be feasible or cost effective to re-key this data into a new application.

On the other hand, if data is in a very complicated format, or is riddled with errors, it may be desirable to re-key the data whilst adopting new software. If this option is selected, it is important to bear in mind the time, cost and resource implications of verifying data after it has been re-keyed. This may be a highly intensive manual operation.

Table 12.1 – Key considerations concerning access to legacy data

Importance	High.
Business Case	Will be dependent on data being accurate and accessible.
Stakeholders	IT staff.
	Business process owners.
	Users with valuable data.
Suggestions for criteria	Has data conversion been proven with a random sample of records?
	Can the new software read the old format without error?

12.3 Data portability

One of the benefits from implementing new software may be making future portability easier. For example, it may be beneficial to increase the effort and cost of data conversion now, to avoid the need for periodic data conversion or re-keying exercises in the future.

There may be a major strategic driver to move towards more future-proof data. For instance, if every new software purchase demands major effort in data conversion, it may be very beneficial to convert all of the data now, thereby reducing future costs. It can be a very sound investment to migrate to a mainstream de facto format, which will be used by software applications for the foreseeable future.

Ongoing technological change is set to deliver entirely new architectures and systems in the next decade or so. Many of these systems will not be widely anticipated now. There has to be considerable benefit in using data formats that are industry standard, rather than using a highly customised format.

> If industry standard formats are used, it is likely that data transfer to a future system will be easier.

12.4 Interface implementation

The interface between new and legacy systems may be implemented through networking, direct hardware or through software. The full details of this will be different on a project-by-project basis. However, in general terms the issues are the same. Where data has to be converted, transferred or migrated, there is always the risk of poor data quality, corruption of records, or slow performance.

Slow performance is a particular problem in software gateways, which may be converting one data format to another (see Figure 12.1). Such gateways must be suitably sized to cope with peaks as well as average loads, and to tackle all the issues associated with data conversion.

For instance, e-mail gateways may be perfectly adequate for occasional traffic transfer between networks; however, they may fail radically if overloaded with large amounts of e-mail at peak times. Gateways may cause so many irritating problems through loss of structured information when transferring e-mails, that the user community becomes unhappy about their use, thus undermining the Business Case.

In all cases where a gateway is involved, it is prudent to fundamentally review the functionality of that gateway, and what will happen to data going from one side to the other and back again as necessary. The flow of data to and fro across the gateway should form a considerable part of any supplier functionality verification exercise and user acceptance testing.

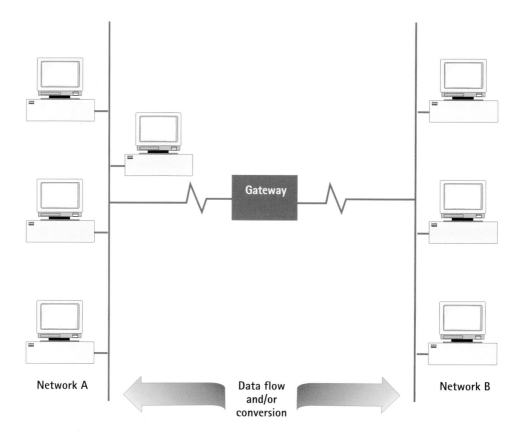

Figure 12.1 – Gateways

Consideration should be given to whether multiple parallel gateways are possible for any new software being purchased. It may be necessary to scale up the performance of a gateway module, and it cannot be assumed that multiple parallel gateways are possible either on the same single machine or across several machines. There may well be constraints on this in the design of the gateway, and this should be clarified with the vendor and supplier as soon as possible in any procurement exercise.

On the plus side, new systems which use de facto data formats or technical interfaces may be able to share data easily between different applications. Data-sharing functions with operating systems can be extremely effective, and have revolutionised the ability to share data between applications with ease.

Availability of a programmable integration capability is also a factor that should be considered. If it is possible to customise data transfer mechanisms using a common programming language, it may be very cost effective to undertake further development. However, if the underlying technologies use specialist programming languages, or require specialist knowledge only available from the supplier, it may not be cost effective or feasible to undertake further work.

The most important point about data transfer between legacy and new systems is to ensure that there is a clear understanding of the business benefits behind what the organisation is trying to do. This provides rational decision-making criteria for what tools to use, and what level of data accuracy to accept.

12.5 Security

All organisations, whether public or private sector, should consider the security implications of new software. Two ways to consider security are:

- internal threats
- external access controls.

Internal threats stem from unauthorised access, misuse of passwords, access or modification of unauthorised data made by people within the organisation. External threats relate to similar issues coming from outside the organisation.

12.5.1 Internal security control

Consideration should be given to the level of security and access control required within the new software. It may be necessary to review requirements against ISO 17799, so that the many different aspects of security are covered.

Choices need to be made in areas such as:

- single or multi-user access
- when, where and why the software may be used, and by whom
- password requirements and rules
- requirements for additional access controls such as ID cards, fingerprint recognition or retina scanning
- encryption of data
- secure printing and control of secure stationery such as cheques
- audit trails and transaction logging requirements
- physical security of access points and data storage.

Many computer operating systems include a rich set of access controls and configuration arrangements that can be used to provide internal security. More stringent requirements will have to be met by other means, such as security controls within the new software application. Such requirements must be clearly stated in the Criteria and Weighting Model.

12.5.2 External security control

All organisations should consider the issues around external data flow and access into and out of their computer systems. The technical details of how a software tool implements remote access and external data flow can be a major weighting factor in the Selection Process.

Areas to consider are:

- e-business initiatives
- firewalls
- dial-in
- e-mail
- mobile telecommunications
- laptops
- data synchronisation.

12.5.2.1 E-business

If the enterprise is engaged in Internet enabling or e-business initiatives, there is likely to be extensive data transfer into and out of the computer systems. Any new software purchase must therefore dovetail with existing initiatives and add value rather than detract from the overall benefits.

> Find the key technical constraints within any e-business initiative, to ensure that any new software purchase is appropriate.
>
> For instance, there are various standards for internal operation of web technologies, and it cannot be assumed that one web service will automatically interface with another.

This area of technology is also changing and developing very quickly. It is necessary to keep up to date with the latest technological developments, and any software purchase should be carefully reviewed by expert technicians. Any detailed technical constraints or criteria should be given high weightings, because if certain technical functions are not fulfilled the software will not work, and the overall benefits will not be achieved.

12.5.2.2 Firewalls

Firewalls and e-mail are significant technical areas that need to work with many new software packages.

Firewalls are specialist computer systems that prevent unauthorised data flows into or out of a computer network. They are a major line of defence against hackers, commercial or national espionage, and inappropriate use of computer equipment by staff. Any new software that communicates across a firewall boundary to a business partner or other organisation must be verified to ensure it will work. There may be certain technical criteria identified by systems architects or security staff, which have very high weight in the Criteria and Weighting Model.

12.5.2.3 External connections

External access is related to firewalls. Some software applications will require external users (whether staff, support or customers) to connect to computer systems. This might be to access data or to use the new software. The security and firewall implications of this must be considered; it is essential to take expert technical advice.

> An Internet banking service modified its log-in security software. Thousands of customers had problems because they were not using up-to-date versions of PC software at home. The help desk quickly became swamped by phone calls and e-mails.
>
> It took several weeks to sort out the mess and there was very bad publicity when it was investigated on national television.

12.5.2.4 E-mail

It is increasingly common for application software to be e-mail enabled. This means that the application is able to send and receive e-mail directly, rather than using a separate piece of e-mail software. Such software must be able to interface with your existing e-mail system.

There may be considerable benefit from migrating to a new software application that uses a different e-mail system. However, it is most important to consider the consequential costs to the rest of the e-mail and organisation, rather than just going ahead with the new software. Most organisations, particularly government and larger private enterprises, have an enormous investment in their e-mail, and any changes to this system or data must be very carefully considered. Technical factors can be very important parts of the overall weighting.

A government organisation wanted to change its e-mail system. The arguments with users over saved copies of previously sent e-mails, storage quotas, archiving etc. were highly contentious.

Many of the users used e-mail for business purposes that the IT people were not aware of, such as archiving and keeping audit trails.

12.5.2.5 Mobile telecommunications

It may be appropriate to consider the increasing use of mobile phones and other hand-held telecommunications devices in relation to a proposed software purchase. Technical telephony criteria, e.g. specific protocol support, may form an important part of the Criteria and Weighting Model.

Introduction of technologies such as WAP may demand significant changes, not just to software, but also to new hardware, telecommunications equipment, security policies, firewalls and all of the related issues.

12.6 Laptops and synchronisation

Related to security is the issue of use of laptops. Many new software packages are purchased to allow staff to use laptops in front of customers or through teleworking from home. This raises all of the security and firewall issues previously discussed.

Also, there is the issue of security and insurance of the laptop itself, including data security. Part of SSP, in particular the Business Case, should be to look at the consequential additional expenditure on insurance and any security devices required to allow software to be used on laptops out of the office.

For instance, it may be a business requirement to use software encryption services, or data encryption services, to ensure that sensitive data cannot be read by anybody who may gain access to or steal a laptop. Costs in this area may be considerable and should therefore form an important part of the Business Case.

Another factor when considering remote data usage or laptops is synchronisation between centralised and remote data.

It will presumably be necessary for remote users with laptops, or a mobile telecomm device, to upload data into the central systems periodically. Changes to data or software updates centrally will also have to be downloaded to the remote devices from time to time (see Figure 12.2).

A company with a large field service staff found it impractical to maintain the laptops over dial-up telephone lines because of the increasing size of software upgrades and patch releases.

Rather than upgrade the communication links, they waited for the field engineers to bring the laptops into the office.

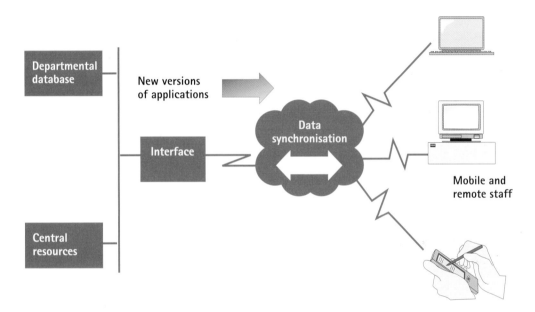

Figure 12.2 – Supporting remote users

The frequency and size of such data transfers must be considered to ensure that appropriate systems, tools, methods and procedures are in place. There may be consequential costs to making this happen, including extra support costs, which must be taken into account in any Business Case for the new software purchase.

Table 12.2 – Key considerations concerning laptops and synchronisation

Importance	Increasingly high.
Business Case	May be closely linked to e-commerce and data sharing. Security threats are a major risk to achievement of benefits and public image.
	Additional insurance costs for laptops.
Approach	Many e-commerce and Internet-related software developments are outsourced.
Stakeholders	Senior managers.
	IT experts.
	Security.
	Commercial people for Internet trading systems.
Suggestions for criteria	Can strategies and policies for security be met?
	What technological criteria must be met?
	What is the impact of new software on existing firewalls?
	What e-mail functions are required?
	What communications functions are required?
	Can existing communications networks cope with the load of supporting laptops?
	Is new encryption software (or hardware) needed?

12.7 Back-up and restore

Consideration should be given to how the new application will be backed up. There are three aspects to this:

- back-up of data
- back-up of the application itself
- back-up of any specialised hardware or peripherals.

In most cases, back-up of these areas will form part of business continuity plans and back-up to the systems as a whole, and there will be no significant change to costs or benefits. However, in other cases, the back-up issues should be considered as part of the criteria for selecting a software application. This is especially true where the application is itself a back-up tool.

Integrity of previous back-ups with old systems must be maintained, and it is unlikely that rival suppliers will fully implement each other's capabilities. It may therefore be necessary to factor into the Business Case the maintenance of a legacy system to maintain the ability to restore old back-ups of legacy data if required. The cost of such a system is likely to rise over time, and raises the issue of when end of life will be declared for legacy data.

Table 12.3 – Key considerations for back-up and restore

Importance	Varies.
Business Case	Costs of maintaining legacy systems for data-restore purposes.
Stakeholders	IT managers.
	Experienced operators.
Suggestions for criteria	Is the back-up regime effective?
	What in-built back-up features are there?
	Can the new software and data be backed up with existing tools?
	Can the new software read the old back-up formats?
	Can individual data sets be restored without restoring the entire back-up?

13
CRITERIA AND WEIGHTING –
ROLL-OUT AND RUN-TIME FACTORS

The costs of rolling out new software may be a major consideration to be factored into the Business Case. There may also be costs incurred in other areas of the organisation.

Roll-out of software can be an extremely expensive and difficult event, demanding large amounts of staff support, and with losses of productivity and working time that may need to be taken into account in the Business Case.

When considering major software purchases, the roll-out methods and tools should be analysed.

> It is one thing to be able to test an application in a single place with a small group of people, it is quite another to be able to implement it across many geographically dispersed sites affecting thousands of people.

There may be technical functions and criteria that must be met so that the new software can be complementary with any existing software distribution and update mechanisms. Technical expertise will be required to define these criteria, set their weighting and make decisions.

13.1 Commonly overlooked costs

There may be considerable costs or other impacts that should be factored into the Business Case. Costs that are often overlooked are:

- disposal costs
- extra systems or networking only needed during roll-out
- contract staff, their equipment and software licences
- roll-out staff expenses and travel costs
- integration work
- bedding-in time and increased support requirements.

A company migrating from mainframe software to UNIX had to dismantle a roof and hire a crane to extract the old mainframe. The crane had to be sited in a busy public car park, so it could only be done at Easter or Christmas.

Table13.1 – Key considerations for commonly overlooked costs

Importance	The bigger the roll-out the more important this is.
Business Case	Should roll-out costs be included?
	Is system downtime a cost?
	Should the disruption to users be considered a cost?
	Should productivity changes, and client impact, be factors?
	The Project Board should check that all areas of cost have been considered.
Stakeholders	Users.
	IT managers.
	Business process owners.
Suggestions for criteria	What important technical criteria must be met?
	How can user disruption be minimised?
	Does the software have features that make roll-out easier, e.g. unattended installation or overnight download?

13.2 Performance and hardware upgrade

Existing hardware, especially PCs, may be perfectly adequate for the current software. However, as soon as a new version or a new application is added to the PC, performance can become unacceptable and the system may even become unreliable.

The additional hardware investment required to bring performance up to an acceptable level is often missed in the Initial Business Case. An effective way to mitigate this risk is to run a realistic user trial as early as possible; this will give early warning of unexpected hardware issues and costs.

Although PCs are becoming steadily more reliable, each major release of software may require even more hardware capability to support it at reasonable speeds. This additional cost must be fully understood during the analysis of the cost benefit of any new software, so that a realistic Business Case is developed.

New software applications may demand much better hardware performance than older applications. It may be necessary to upgrade the hardware before the software can be used.

It is also the case that, as for increasing demands on memory, increasing demands on other functions of computer hardware are fairly normal with each new release of software. There may therefore be a case to upgrade hardware, in parallel with arrival of new applications.

The Business Case for purchasing software should include any relevant hardware costs.

Purchase of software is an opportunity to achieve additional business benefit through changing hardware.

There may be knock-on hardware costs that were not originally envisaged.

The principle areas of run-time technical requirements to be considered are:

- disk space
- memory
- screens
- networking
- printers
- specialist peripherals.

13.2.1 Disk space

Recent hardware developments have increased disk size exponentially. Whereas availability of disk space was a major constraint a few years ago, even entry-level PCs have the disk capacity that mainframe computers had ten years ago.

13.2.2 Memory

Generally speaking, the less memory installed, the fewer things a computer can do simultaneously, and performance bottlenecks may occur. The cost of memory in computers has now fallen to a very low level and is no longer an effective constraint to software functionality.

It is now common for each purchase of a new release of software to make vastly increased memory demands on a computer. This may in turn cause performance problems, or make the software run with the equivalent of a car handbrake pulled on.

The capacity of RAM available in computers is rising exponentially, and the cost is also falling. However, each new version of many software tools and applications seems to require more and more memory. It is therefore quite likely that RAM upgrades will be required, certainly for mission-critical software, and these costs should be taken into account.

13.2.3 Screens

The development of high-resolution screens at reasonable cost has made new opportunities for software designers, and software users may get major benefit from using a higher quality, higher resolution screen.

A new software application may require the purchase of a new screen for a PC. Technical developments will lead to smaller footprints, increased clarity and better video performance.

Newer versions of software tend to have more menus, toolbars and other functions visible. Software may even be written assuming a large format screen will be used. There may be a health and safety issue in terms of replacing older screens with newer, larger ones, to ensure that staff do not suffer excessive eye strain when using new applications.

13.2.4 Network

Network functionality is increasingly part of the architecture of software applications. Changes to software applications may impact:

- local area networks
- wide area networks
- intranets
- extranets
- World Wide Web
- specialised networks and connectivity.

It is important to consider the impact of new software on network loading, both internally and externally. Capacity planning people within the IT community should be involved in setting criteria and developing a rounded Business Case.

New software may bring significant new network demands, through larger file size, increased file sharing or data transfer, or new communications functions. The impact of these should be understood, and any criteria or weightings set as appropriate. There may be additional costs that have to be built into the Business Case, for instance, higher speed telephone lines or upgraded internal networks.

The impact of a new application may be very large even though the amount of data being transferred is very small. This is particularly true where there are large numbers of users. For instance, a lot of users each transferring a little bit of data regularly can cause a very significant increase to network load. The important point to remember is to be aware of all of the consequences of the software purchase to ensure that the Business Case genuinely is valid.

> A government department introduced PC software to poll a server every minute to check for updated bulletin board messages. When it went live on 500 PCs, the Ethernet local area network became swamped, and the server performance dropped off dramatically.

The more sophisticated or distributed a software application is, the more likely that a software change will impact a network. Corporate grade network hardware can be very expensive, easily adding millions of euros of extra cost. Clearly the full implications of new software must be understood, with expert input from systems architects and network experts.

13.2.5 Printers

The impact on printers should also be considered. Printing is often overlooked as a factor in software selection.

The primary output of many applications still remains a piece of paper. Even in these enlightened Internet-enabled days, much information is still structured around documents that have to be printed from time to time. If these printing mechanisms are not fully effective and reasonably swift, user dissatisfaction grows very rapidly and major loss of productivity can result.

> Efficiency of printing should be a prime consideration in any software procurement, and should be tested and proven **before** implementation.
>
> An Internet banking service changed their statement printing systems at the same time as changing their customer log-in security. Both new systems failed to work perfectly first time, leading to swamped help desk and support staff, and weeks of bad publicity and chaos. The two technical problems compounded each other as customers tried all ways to get data about their accounts.

It may also be the case that new printer functionality is required. For instance, if the new application introduces high accuracy graphics then it will probably also be necessary to introduce high accuracy graphic printing.

Colour printing may also be required. Where there are large numbers of users this may be a considerable extra expense above and beyond the cost of the software itself.

13.2.6 Specialist peripherals

Many software applications, e.g. scientific applications, include functions that use specialised peripherals such as data loggers, sensors, controls or robotic machinery. Obviously, any new software must be evaluated in the light of the whole system rather than only the software element.

13.3 Integration

It is very risky to assume that systems from the same manufacturer will interface smoothly first time. In many cases different generations of systems will not be designed to work perfectly together, even though marketing literature may imply that they do.

> Project plans that include short duration tasks, such as two days for integration, should be treated with scepticism until proved otherwise.
>
> A considerable part of the cost of implementation with new software can be in resolving integration problems and reducing errors to an acceptable level. This is a very common cause of escalating implementation costs and user dissatisfaction.

It is easy to ignore or underestimate this cost in a Business Case. A recommended strategy is to get suppliers to prove the integration capabilities before committing to the purchase.

Live operational environments are likely to be far more complicated, and contain far more faulty data and other challenges, than the test systems used by software or IT developers. It is dangerous to assume that technical interfaces in software are going to work reliably and predictably without extended bedding-in time. This should be factored into the Business Case, so that benefits are realistic rather than instant.

13.3.1 Interface verification

It is prudent to ensure that sufficient definition and testing are done on any new software. For major new software applications this should be done before purchase to ensure that all key interfaces will:

- work at the right speeds
- preserve data quality
- be easy to use.

Failure to do this may result in an application which is difficult to use, or unreliable. The new application could become an island of data, thereby losing large amounts of business value from the new system.

13.4 Standards for user-programmable languages

Although some de facto and international standards are emerging, there are still many areas of software technology where incompatible competing standards still exist. This is especially true of the innovative and very new areas of development such as the Internet, World Wide Web, and telecommunications. For instance, there is a range of scripting languages, widely used within Internet servers and Internet software applications, which do not necessarily work together.

Scripting languages have comparable functionality in World Wide Web services, but are not identical. Each has its own strengths, weaknesses and operational constraints. It is therefore imperative to get an understanding of what a business group needs from its scripting software, and that all of the technical criteria identified by technicians are met. Once again, expert technical advice will be required, and senior technical interests represented at the decision-making level.

There is also the possibility that valuable new software functions are required by the business, and this may cause new web server software to be introduced as a consequence. Such costs must be taken into account in the Business Case.

APPENDIX A – GLOSSARY

This section lists the meanings of frequently used terms within this book. This glossary is derived from the PRINCE2® glossary of terms which is widely used and accepted.

Acceptance criteria
A prioritised list of criteria that the final product(s) must meet before the customer will accept them; a measurable definition of what must be done for the final product to be acceptable.

Benefits
The positive outcomes, quantified or unquantified, that the software is required to deliver, and that justify the investment.

Benefits realisation
The practice of ensuring that the outcome of a project produces the projected benefits claimed in the Business Case.

Business Case
Information that describes the justification for buying the new software. It provides the reasons (and answers the question 'Why?') for the project. It is updated at key points.

Peer review
Peer reviews are specific reviews of a project or any of its products where personnel from within the organisation and/or from other organisations carry out an independent assessment of the project. Peer reviews can be done at any point within a project but are often used at stage-end points.

Phase
A part, section or segment of a project, similar in meaning to a PRINCE2 stage. The key meaning of stage in PRINCE2 terms is the use of management stages, i.e. sections of the project to which the Project Board only commits one at a time. A phase might be more connected to a time slice, change of skills required or change of emphasis.

PRINCE2
A method that supports some selected aspects of project management. The acronym stands for **PR**ojects **IN** Controlled Environments.

PRINCE2 project
A project whose product(s) can be defined at its start sufficiently precisely so as to be

measurable against predefined metrics and that is managed according to the PRINCE2 method.

Process
That which must be done to bring about a particular outcome, in terms of information to be gathered, decisions to be made and results that must be achieved.

Programme
A portfolio of projects selected, planned and managed in a co-ordinated way.

Project
A temporary organisation that is created for the purpose of delivering one or more business products according to a specified Business Case.

Project management
The planning, monitoring and control of all aspects of the project and the motivation of all those involved in it to achieve the project objectives on time and to the specified cost, quality and performance.

Project Manager
The person given the authority and responsibility to manage the project on a day-to-day basis to deliver the required products within the constraints agreed with the Project Board.

Quality
The totality of features and characteristics of a product or service that bear on its ability to satisfy stated and implied needs. Also defined as 'fitness for purpose' or 'conforms to requirements'.

Quality Management System
The complete set of quality standards, procedures and responsibilities for a site or organisation.

Quality review
A quality review is a quality checking technique with a specific structure, defined roles and procedure designed to ensure a product's completeness and adherence to standards. The participants are drawn from those with an interest in the product and those with the necessary skills to review its correctness. An example of the checks made by a quality review is 'Does the document match the quality criteria in the Product Description?'

Quality system
See Quality Management System.

Request for Change
A means of proposing a modification to the current specification of a product.

Reviewer
A person asked to review a product that is the subject of a quality review.

Senior Responsible Owner
This is not a PRINCE2 term, but is used in many organisations. Its equivalent in PRINCE2 terms would be the 'Executive' role.

Senior Supplier
The Project Board role that provides knowledge and experience of the main discipline(s) involved in the production of the project's deliverable(s). Represents the supplier(s) interests within the project and provides supplier resources.

Senior User
A member of the Project Board, accountable for ensuring that user needs are specified correctly and that the solution meets those needs.

Sponsor
Not a specific PRINCE2 role but often used to mean the major driving force of a project. May be the equivalent of Executive or corporate/programme management.

Stakeholders
Parties with an interest in the execution and outcome of a project. They would include business streams affected by or dependent on the outcome of a project.

Supplier
The group or groups responsible for the supply of the project's specialist products.

Team Manager
A role that may be employed by the Project Manager or a specifically appointed alternative person to manage the work of project team members.

User
The person or group who will use the final deliverable(s) of the project.

APPENDIX B – FURTHER INFORMATION

APM Group Ltd
Administers the Management of Risk (M_o_R), Managing Successful Programmes (MSP), and Managing Successful Projects (PRINCE2) methodologies on behalf of OGC.

7–8 Queen Square
High Wycombe
Buckinghamshire
HP11 2BP

Telephone: 01494 452450
Fax: 01494 459559
Website: http://www.prince2.org.uk

Office of Government Commerce (OGC)
The UK Government's centre of excellence for business practices. An office of HM Treasury, producing a wide range of management guidance for the public sector, and responsible for bringing together the Management of Risk (M_o_R), Managing Successful Programmes (MSP), and Managing Successful Projects (PRINCE2) methodologies.

Rosebery Court
St Andrews Business Park
Norwich
NR7 0HS

Telephone: +44 (0)845 000 4999
E-mail: servicedesk@ogc.gov.uk
Website: http://www.ogc.gov.uk

The Turnbull Report
Now known colloquially as 'The Turnbull Report', this report was part of the Combined Code for control and governance of Stock Exchange listed companies. Researched and published by Nigel Turnbull of the Institute of Chartered Accountants, it provides authoritative guidance on risk management and internal control.

Internal Control – Guidance for Directors on the Combined Code
September 1999 ISBN 1 84152 010 1

Published by:
The Institute of Chartered Accountants in England and Wales
Chartered Accountants' Hall
PO Box 433
Moorgate Place
London EC2P 2BJ

INDEX

Note: References to tables are denoted by *italic* type; references to figures are denoted by **bold** type.